INEVITABLE

A Celebration of LIFE, LABOR, LOVE

(REVISED EDITION)

INEVITABLE

A Celebration of LIFE, LABOR, LOVE

(REVISED EDITION)

JEROME G. FARRIS

CITI OF BOOKS

CITIOFBOOKS, INC.
3736 Eubank NE Suite A1
Albuquerque, NM 87111-3579
www.citiofbooks.com
Hotline: 1 (877) 389-2759
Fax: 1 (505) 930-7244

Ordering Information:
Quantity sales. Special discounts are available on quantity purchases by corporations, associations, and others. For details, contact the publisher at the address above.

Printed in the United States of America.

ISBN-13:   Softcover   978-1-963209-54-9
                eBook   978-1-963209-55-6

Library of Congress Control Number: 2024902078

TABLE OF CONTENTS

INEVITABLE

A Celebration of Life, Labor Love

Foreword by Yolanda Farris

I am in awe of God. The gift of a shared life with my husband has been the vital source on my path of healing. Prior to meeting Jerome, I was broken and seeking to be made whole. I needed to completely surrender my life to God. In a state of sadness and deep depression, I prayed to God and asked him, "Lord what would you have me do, and how may I serve you?

As I prayed to God, I maintained a posture of stillness. While I became still, I cleared my tears and waited on Him. Then, after much prayer, I was given direction and purpose to serve as a volunteer at the Open Door Rescue Mission. I had no idea that this experience would alter the course of my life. I would not have imagined being married to such a man of faith.

Jerome found me (Proverb 18:22) and has been used by God in this quest for wholeness. During this journey, I appreciate the patience and incredible love of God that I have experienced through Jerome.

To witness his commitment to the call on his life in serving God has been a tremendous inspiration to me. I have learned to sacrifice my own desires and wants in order to do God's will.

There are challenges in life, however, how we answer them define who we are. As I faced many tests and trails, so has my husband, not only through grief and loss but also in ministry. Jerome's example of steadfast, unwavering faith, and trust in God has helped us overcome them all. We know God is in control and that He has a plan for our lives. I have been blessed to see God's power, deliverance, and grace firsthand in our lives as He has brought us together as one in fulfilling His divine purpose, living a life of service.

My prayer is that you will begin to see the hand of God at work in your life, that you will trust His voice, and yield to His will. The life God has planned for us is far better than we could have imagined. May this book inspire you to seek God's face and trust His divine path for your life (Jeremiah 29:11)

For You, art my lamp, O Lord: The Lord shall enlighten my darkness. For by You I have run against a troop: By my God I can leap over a wall. As for God, His way is perfect; The word of the Lord is proven: He is a shield to all who trust Him.

For who is God, except the Lord? And who is a rock, except our God? God is my strength and power: And He makes my way perfect. He makes my feet like the feet of deer, and sets me on my high places.
2 Samuel 22: 29-3

"In memory of my son Dion, my Wild Card. You played the hand that you were dealt in life. You kept the most important card for last and received the ultimate prize, your home in glory. Well done my son."

This book is dedicated to you.

The steps of a good man are
ordered by the Lord:
and he delighteth in his way
Psalm 37:23

INTRODUCTION

This book is a tribute and testimony to God and His promise to all that would trust Him to fulfill His word and will in their life. Little did I know that the year 2020 would bring with it many of the promises God made to me in fulfilling my calling, purpose, and dreams.

> *Life is filled with swift transitions, naught of earth unmoved can stand, build your hopes on things eternal, hold to God's unchanging hand.*
> *(W. Oliver Cooper – 1885)*

Because I believe God, trust Him, and have not let go of His hand, I can truly say God is faithful and will do what He says. This is a journey of the last 10 years of my life. As you walk with me, let me confess right now that I could neither have planned what I will share with you nor made it up myself. I am simply not smart enough.

BUT GOD! This is what I mean:

On October 16, 2009, in my first book, *God's Purpose for My Pain,* I wrote about a time in my life that began with devastation, indescribable pain, and grief after the death of my beloved wife, Helene, but ended with a sense of great expectation and hope for a wonderful future that God had planned for me.

Exactly to the day on October 16, 2019, I was awakened by God and moved by His Spirit to begin this book. In it, I wish to share with you how over the last 10 years, God has divinely ordered my steps to this place I am now in, a place of awe in Him *"doing exceedingly, abundantly more than I could have asked or imagined according to the power that worketh within* me." (Ephesians 3:20) What was promised to me has been performed far beyond what I could have imagined or tried to do myself, hence forth the title, INEVITABLE.

When you look at the word "inevitable" what may come to mind are terms such as predictable, expected, foreseeable, preordained, or predestined. Simply put, God said: ***"I've got plans for you, plans to prosper you and not to harm you, plans to give you hope and a future. (Jeremiah 29:11 - paraphrased)***

Because God's plans, thoughts, and ways are not ours, He will do and allow things to take place in our lives that we may not like, are uncomfortable with, and in some cases would rather avoid. In other words: ***"God will take you where you need to go in order for you to become what He wants you to be."*** [1]

Some might call it fate, I have chosen to call it my "*destiny.*" God has divinely orchestrated three milestone events in my life for the year 2020. I have labeled them as "A Celebration of ***LIFE, LABOR, and***

LOVE." Look for a moment at the following numbers: 60, 30, and 10. If I may transpose them a little deeper "010360."

MY LIFE .... It was <u>60 years ago</u> on January 3, 1960, that I was seen in the mind of God, placed in the womb of my mother, Levolia, and born into this world. *"I knew you before I formed you in your mother's womb." (Jeremiah 1:5a)*

MY LABOR .... It was <u>30 years ago</u> in April of 1990 that I was ordained as a minister of the gospel of Jesus Christ. I later became a missionary and director of Open Door Rescue Mission and pastor of Open Door Gospel Tabernacle (both in Detroit Michigan), having now served 30 years of ministry for my Lord Jesus Christ. *"Before you were born, I set you apart and appointed you as my prophet to the nations." (Jeremiah 1:5b)*

MY LOVE .... It will be <u>10 years ago,</u> Lord's will, on October 23, 2020, that what God had promised me will come to pass. Even though Helene, the one whom I had loved since I was a teen was now gone, I would love again. I have been blessed with the most remarkable, loving, giving, help meet: my queen, Yolanda.

Don't go too fast. I was not looking for a wife 10 years ago. I kid you not. God literally brought her to me. He knew what I would need in order to carry out His will in the future, so He gave me this precious gift.

Again, BUT GOD!

God, from the beginning of creation has a design for every area of our lives. This "design" is that we would be prosperous not necessarily in material or earthly things but spiritually through our inheritance we have with Jesus Christ. He wants and desires this for us because we are His children; however, it does not just happen. God gives us a choice. One must choose to be in covenant with Him. By choosing to be in this relationship, yielding to His will and not your own, you will delight in Him, and God promises to give you the desire of your heart. (Psalm 37:4) I will speak on this revelation later in chapter 9.

This is my life, ordered by God. My prayer is that the promises God has for you will be realized in yours as well.

Notes

1. See the author's book, God's Purpose for My Pain (ASA Publishing 2010, page 106)

LIFE

For I know the thoughts I have toward you, saith the Lord; thoughts of peace, and not of evil, to give you an expected end.

Jeremiah 29:11

1

Get Ready For Your Destiny

Everything that happens to you in life is preparing you for something, an opportunity that will come. How you begin does not have to be how you end. So many believe that where they are, is where they will forever be, that the current environment or circumstance determines their future. This simply is not true.

In the final chapter of my book God's Purpose for My Pain, I shared with you just how far God brought me from that dark day of loss, how the wound, so deep in my heart, had miraculously healed from within, and that a scar remained as a reminder to me of what a precious jewel I had in my love, my life, my Clair.

I thought the writing was done, but God was not finished with me. There was still much He needed to show me: I needed to make plans for my life. I was about to do some things I had never imagined: meet people I would bless and be blessed by, and touch lives far beyond my comprehension.

He showed me that when it comes to destiny, we can embrace it or remain where we are. With God there are no ceilings on our life, obstacles that cannot be overcome, or barriers that can stand in our way. No matter what may come, it's in God's plan, and *"those who love him, and are the called according to purpose, know it will work out for their good." (Romans 8:28)*

I could not and would not allow the pain of where I was, steal my vision and destiny. I learned through that time with God to not waste my valleys and that He was positioning me for later divine appointments. What was done for others He would do for me. We see in scripture that ….

It was not by chance but destiny, that a Jewish baby by the name of Moses was placed in the Nile River, raised in the house of Pharaoh as an Egyptian, and would become the deliverer of His people Israel. (Exodus 2:1 – 2:10)

It was not by chance but destiny, that a young man was born blind, not because of sins that he or his parents might have committed, but because Jesus would be coming by on that day in order that the power of God would be witnessed by all who were present. (John 9:1-3)

It was not by chance but destiny, that a young boy would die, but on his way to the graveyard in the funeral procession be raised from the dead by Jesus and given back to his mother, who was a widow. (Luke 7:11-17)

<u>It was not by chance but destiny</u>, that a woman, who had for 18 years suffered with an infirmity that caused her to walk bowed down, was able to walk upright after meeting the man from Galilee. (Luke 13:10-17)

<u>It was not by chance but destiny,</u> that a fish would be the first UPS carrier that would deliver the money needed in order that the disciples could pay their taxes. (Matthew 17:24-27)

<u>It was not by chance but destiny,</u> that the servant of a centurion soldier would suddenly, after feeling sick and near death, miraculously feel healing and strength – no doctor in sight but simply because of a word of healing spoken from the Balm of Gilead. (Matthew 8:5-13)

<u>It was not by chance but destiny,</u> that a certain man would be asked for the use of his donkey that had never been ridden before but that Jesus would be the first, as He would ride it into the streets of Jerusalem. (Matthew 21:1-3)

<u>It was not by chance but destiny,</u> that on one particular day, that seemed like any other day for 38 long years, a lame man who had been coming to a pool in hopes of being thrown in first and physically healed, would be made whole because he met Jesus. (John 5:5)

<u>It was destiny</u> that a crippled man was visited by four friends who knew that if they could get him in to see Jesus, he would be able to walk again. (Mark 2:1-12)

<u>It was destiny</u> that the virtue of Jesus would temporarily leave Him simply because of the faith of a woman's outstretched hands touching the hem of His garment. (Mark 5:25-34)

<u>It was destiny</u> that a young Jewish lad, who participated in the stoning of one of the first deacons of the church, would later become the greatest of the apostles, even though he considered himself to be the least of them all. (Acts 7:58)

<u>It was destiny</u> that Jesus waited a few days after hearing that His friend, Lazarus, had died that He would allow Lazarus's death to be the subject of the lesson that He is the resurrection and the life.

"I am the resurrection and the life: he that believeth in me,
though he were dead, yet shall he live;
And whosoever liveth and believeth
in me shall never die".
John 11: 25-26

It had become a part of my destiny .... That on August 5, 2009, after 28 wonderful years with an amazing woman as my wife, God decided to call her home, leaving me to continue my journey and fulfill my purpose for Him.

Not as though I have already attained, either were
already perfect; but I follow after, if I may apprehend
that which
I am apprehended of Christ Jesus.

Brethren, I count not myself to have apprehended;
but this one thing I do, forgetting those things
which are behind, and reaching forth unto those
things which are before I press toward the mark
for the prize of the high calling
of God in Christ
Jesus.
Philippians 3: 12-14:

That was 14 years ago. This is now. I have fortified my faith by releasing the promises of God into my life. Every promise He has made concerning my destiny is being established and coming to pass. As we begin this journey together, realize …

It's never too late to become what you might have been. 1

Notes

1. "Literary News: A Monthly Journey of Current Literature," 1881 George Eliot

LIFE

It isn't what you are that holds you back, it's what you believe you are not.
Denis Waitley

2

THE CHOICE IS YOURS

God has a plan in mind for all who have placed their trust in Him. The Word of God supports this belief:

*Jeremiah 29:11 – "**For I know the thoughts (plans) I have toward you,** saith the Lord; thoughts of peace, and not of evil, to give you an expected end."*

*Ephesians 2:10 – "For we are his workmanship, created in Christ Jesus unto good works, **which God hath before ordained that we should walk in them."***

*Hebrews 12:1 – "Wherefore seeing we also are compassed about with so great a cloud of witnesses, let us lay aside every weight, and the sin … run with endurance the race God has set which doth so easily beset us, **and let us run with patience the race that is set before us."***

These plans God has for us are to be discovered and then carried out. They can only be carried out through being intentional and through cooperation with God. God's plan or "destiny" for us is totally different than what the world believes about destiny. Webster defines destiny as **"the predetermined or inevitable course of events considered beyond the power or control of people."** Even though there may be some truth in this statement, it falls short of biblical destiny.

For example, John 3:16 says, *"For God so loved the world that he gave his only begotten son that whosoever believeth in him shall not perish but have everlasting life."* The whosoever says that not all will believe. The reason all will not accept the gift of salvation is because man has the free will (or contrary to Webster's definition the "power and control") to choose whether he or she wants it or not. Here is God's desire:

The Lord is not slack concerning his promise, as some men count slackness but is longsuffering us-ward, not willing that any should perish but that all might come to repentance."
2 Peter 3:9

What God desires possibly will not be manifested in a person's life because that person has a responsibility. The responsibility is to embrace what God has done solely based on his grace.

For by grace are ye saved through faith and that not of yourselves: it is a gift of God: not of works, lest any man should boast....
Ephesians 2:8

You can live outside of God's will and never reach your full potential; therefore, when it comes to our destiny, we have a responsibility to discover God's will for us and then to walk in it. Paul said to the saints in Ephesus…

> I therefore, the prisoner of the Lord, beseech you that ye walk
> worthy of the vocation wherewith ye are called.
> Ephesians 4:1

Make no mistake, our eternal destiny is set if we have accepted Jesus as our Lord and Savior. There is nothing that we can do to change that, for we have been sealed with the Holy Spirit of promise. (Ephesians 1:14)

What I am sharing regarding destiny is your appointed time while here on earth, fulfilling the purpose God had in mind for you that He might get glory through your life now. Because we *have choices in life,* we can choose living by design or living by default. Living a life God had planned for us or living a settle-for life. Being complacent with average or taking on the challenge to be the best "you" for God.

Start where you are with what you have.
Make something out of it and never be satisfied.
George Washington Carver

If a person becomes content with average, he or she will rarely exert the work and effort for excellence. The longer you remain satisfied in life the less likely you will challenge yourself to become more. Now there is a difference between complacency (settling) and contentment. To be complacent means to show uncritical satisfaction for oneself or one's achievement, to be smug, unbothered.

**If you won't be better tomorrow than you are today,
then what do you need tomorrow for?
Rabbi Nachman of Breslov**

On the other hand, to be content means to be in a state of peace. Are you at peace with God and the plan He has for your life? To be at peace with God is *"to have made the choice"* to receive His son, Jesus, into your life.

Therefore, being justified by faith, we have peace with God through our Lord Jesus Christ. By whom also we have access by faith into the grace wherein we stand, and rejoice in the hope of the glory of God Romans 5:1-2

To be content with what's happening in your life now is to know that God is at work (because He has a plan in mind for you), regardless of your situation, and that you are committed to working hard in glorifying and pleasing Him while waiting on Him.

The Apostle Paul was content (at peace with) whatever state he found himself in at that moment:

"Not that I speak in respect of want: for I learned, in whatsoever state I am therewith to be content".
Philippians 4:11

Why could Paul be content wherever state he found himself in? The reason is because he could see life from God's point of view. He focused on what he was supposed to do and not what he should have. I need to say that again in case you didn't get it. ***"He focused on what he was supposed to be doing and not what he should have."*** There were certain periods in his life when it was God's will for him to be there, and that was fine with him.

This is not an easy concept to accept. Many people can have the tendency to feel entitled, thinking they deserve something. I must confess, for a moment I was one of them. I had to learn that God owes me nothing. When one becomes so focused on what they think they should receive, they can miss the satisfaction in knowing that they did the best they could do.

We can have a tendency to confuse worldly success with godly success. Worldly success is short-sighted and, if followed, ends in misery, but biblical success is spiritual, lasting, and ends in eternal life and joy. Whereas worldly success is centered on the promotion and gratification of ourselves, biblical success is centered on obedience to and glorification of God. This was my truth, and for a moment I was very discouraged and depressed.

Have you reached the point where you tried and tried and the more you tried, it seemed like the more you failed? Have you ever felt like you were getting nowhere? Have you ever given words of encouragement and inspiration and it seemed like no sooner that it left your mouth and got to one ear, it went out the other? Have you ever been there where the more you try to reach higher the further you sink? And, sometimes have you just felt like giving up? This is where I was, and I felt like it wasn't even worth it, but I thank God today for friends who were there for me.

No one knows what a pastor goes through except another pastor. Thank you to Pastor Jim Jones, a seasoned pastor of over 50 years, who opened his home, spent hours with me at his dining room table listening to my frustrations, and shared with me how God has helped him.

Thank you to Pastor Kevin Butcher, a servant whose heart is toward ministering to pastors. He helped me realize that I was not alone and that God was pleased with my service, love, and commitment to his people. *"To not be weary in well doing for I would reap if I fainted not."*

And thank you to my brother, Pastor Arthur Willis, who in his unique way reminded me that this was not about me and what I wanted, but about God and his Kingdom. I thank God for restoring the joy of my salvation.

For those of you who have been given the call on your life to serve and may have experienced depression that comes at times with the weight and burden of ministry, know that you are not alone and that there is someone who can help you. The prophet Jeremiah understood what it felt like.

In Jeremiah chapter 20, he felt like quitting, but there was something within that wouldn't let him do it. I discovered, as Jeremiah did, that I needed a better understanding from God's perspective what ministry and "Kingdom Work" was all about. We need to clear our perception about God's plan.

In Matthew 6:10 when you pray, always pray "thy will." The Greek meaning for "thy will" is "plan." What Jesus was saying in this model prayer is that when we pray, always put in there a surrender and submission to God's own schedule. Sometimes God's schedule for us is not a schedule that takes you through sunshiny days.

Sometimes that schedule accounts for some dark clouds and proverbial thunder, lighting, and tough winds. Not always up, it's sometimes down. Not always good, it's sometimes bad.

Jeremiah's complaint to God was: you tricked me, you deceived me, you took advantage because you're bigger than me, and everybody is laughing at me. I wanted to turn in my preaching license, pull off my clergy collar, take my robe off, clean out my library, pack my sermons, and tell the church I'm done, but then something started to burn from within and just wouldn't let me do it.

If our perception is to be clear about God's plan, we need to understand that sainthood does not stop you from suffering.

Man, that is born of a woman is of a few days and those
days are full of trouble.
Job 14:1

Jesus said that in this world you will have tribulations
but be of good cheer for I have
overcome the world.
John 16:33

Through much prayer, repentance, and soul searching I learned these valuable lessons and gained a greater appreciation of God for what He had willed for my life. I embraced this state of contentment, and because of it, I began to find greater purpose. In discovering that purpose, I needed to get closer to God.

In the summer of 2012, after 22 years of service, I resigned as the director of the Open-Door Rescue Mission. Deep down within me burned a passion: I knew there was more that God wanted me to do. I didn't know exactly what it was, but I felt it. I always want to do more and be more for God, to grow, develop, and become all I could be to His glory. I intentionally embraced the thought that God was not finished with me and that He would reveal what that would look like. While waiting on Him, there were more valuable lessons I would learn.

I believed that the God who saved me also heard my cry.

For years I had prayed to God about an "issue of pride" I had, and God had seemed silent. I did not realize that He was *"working it out of me."* It seemed that He was silent, but all the time He was demonstrating his love and mercy towards me when I had doubts and insecurities.

He who did not spare his own Son, but gave him up for us
all how will he not also with him graciously
give us all things.
Romans 8:32

In other words, the cross is our guarantee that God is for us and is committed to giving us everything we would ask for according to His will. He desires more for us than we can comprehend. We can be content with that and wait patiently for His answers.

I watched with expectancy, although not prepared for the unexpected answers.

In the morning, LORD, you hear my voice
in the morning I lay my requests
before you and wait expectantly.
Psalm 5:3

While God has been faithful to answer many of my prayers, it's often been in far different ways than I would have anticipated! Sometimes what we look for and desire is not what we need or what He wills for us. The only way to do what He and I both wanted, at times, would involve various degrees of discomfort in my life. Again, *He will take you where you need to go in order for you to become what He wants you to be.*

Growing in humility means pride has to be done away with. Learning to love like Jesus requires us to say no to self's constant demand for selfish ambition, wanting our own way, and putting ourselves first. Growing in patience inevitably involves some form of waiting. When we lay our requests before Him, it is by faith that we wait and watch in anticipation for God's good work in us and others. While waiting, God gives you the strength you need.

> They that wait upon the Lord shall renew their strength
> They shall mount with wings as an eagle
> they shall run and not be weary
> they shall walk and not faint.
> Isaiah 40:31

I had to put more hope in His Word

We can be tempted to put our hope in things that may disappoint us in the end. We can hope a doctor will heal us, a teacher will pass us, a spouse will love us, our employer will reward us, or a friend will help us. But it is only when we put our hope in Christ that we can wait with confidence and know we will not be put to shame.

> I wait for the LORD, my soul doth wait, and in his word do I hope
> My soul waiteth for the Lord more than they that watch
> for the morning: I say, more than they that
> watch for the morning.
> Psalm 130: 3-5

It's clear to me that God allows us to experience disappointments in life to teach us that nothing else will truly satisfy or provide us with a firm foundation to stand upon. God's Word alone is that foundation.

We can wait for the Lord knowing that, no matter how dark the night is, His light will breakthrough in our lives, bringing abundant joy through a more intimate relationship with Christ.

"The darkest nights produce the brightest stars."
John Green

I trusted more in the Lord, and not my own understanding

Why is it so tempting for us to depend on our own wisdom rather than the wisdom of our all-wise God? What makes us think that we know better than He does what is best for us? Scripture speaks clearly about how to live life abundantly forever with Christ; yet, all too easily, we justify our sin and do what is right in our own eyes. It is the seasons of waiting that reveal where we are placing our trust.

I <u>eventually</u> resisted worrying, refrained from anger, became still, and chose to be patient.

> Be still before the LORD and wait patiently for him
> do not fret when people succeed in their ways
> when they carry out their wicked schemes
> Refrain from anger and turn from wrath
> do not fret-it leads only to evil.
> Psalm 37: 7-8

This took for me a while to get. It's easy to say we trust God, but our response to delays, frustrations, and difficult situations exposes where we are actually placing our hope.

Are we convinced God is listening? Do we believe He's good? Do we accept that our circumstances are sovereignly ordained? Do we doubt He really cares about us? *As we choose* to wait quietly and trustingly, we not only honor God but also encourage others to put their hope in Him as well.

Through the years God was revealing these many truths to me, I also began to further develop myself. As much as we may want something to happen, it just doesn't happen. It's like what a farmer must do. He must plan and put in the effort to plant. He must cultivate and fertilize. If he does his part, God will give the increase. If he doesn't act with diligence, God can't, or more accurately, won't. God is able to do all things, but then there are some things He leaves for us to do. His desire is to work through us.

Within each of us is a gift God has given. It's called potential. Our gift to God is to develop it. The sky is the limit on what a person is capable of accomplishing with God's help. Paul said in Philippians 4:19, ***"I can do all things through Christ who strengthens me."*** I understood that to mean to be more and do more for God. I had to become a better me. Growth was essential in order to maximize my potential. I began making a concerted effort to spend more time with God on a consistent basis.

> As newborn babes desire the sincere
> milk of the word that ye may grow thereby
> 1 Peter 2:2

In God's Purpose for My Pain, I entitled one of the chapters "Running on Empty." It marked a period of time when a member of my church was looking to his pastor for consolation due to the death of his friend, Helene, my wife. I had nothing to give. During that time, I also had a preaching engagement at another church and really was not "feeling it", but Dad, Pastor Robert Ware, a spiritual father and mentor, shared with me that he had experienced the exact same thing losing his first wife. He said to me, "Son, I know you are hurting, but the people need a word from you." All I can say is…

BUT GOD!

As always, God was faithful and blessed me with what I needed to fulfill my calling and purpose to preach His word that day. Vital lessons learned on this journey is that you cannot give what you don't have and cannot help others if you have not been helped.

In the summer of 2016, I felt this emptiness again emotionally, mentally, and spiritually. As pastors, we have a reservoir stored up to bless and meet the needs of those whom God has given us to serve. However, sometimes that supply will become depleted and we may find our ministry suffering because we are not the best we can be for God, let alone for others. I shared this with my church family, stressing my need to be replenished. It was at this time that I "*intentionally*" began my journey and commitment of self-development and personal growth.

**"Opportunity is missed by most people
because it is dressed up in overalls
and it looks like work."**
Anonymous

We don't always take advantage of opportunities we have because they don't come dressed like we thought they should.

**"The only place SUCCESS comes before
WORK is in the dictionary".**
Arthur Brisbane

We have to intentionally look for opportunities if we are to catch them. They will only come if we are prepared to receive them. Preparation comes when we are committed to growing and becoming better.

You Cannot Become If You Are Too Attached
to What You Have Been

LIFE

Growth is the only guarantee that
tomorrow is going to get better.
John Maxwell

3

YOU MUST BE INTENTIONAL

To be intentional you must *"want to make a difference."*

Every person wants his or her life to matter. One of my favorite movies during the Christmas season is *It's a Wonderful Life* with Jimmy Stewart. Most of you know the story of George Bailey, believing his life was meaningless and would have been better if he had not been born. He later discovers that his life did matter and he did make a difference in the lives of others.

No matter what plot has been played in your life, your life matters, and if you are reading this book, there are still blank pages to your story. You have the ability to fill them with God's help. People often lose hope, joy, and a sense of purpose in life because they have lost sight of God and do not actively, *intentionally*, and purposefully pursue what He has planned for them. We don't follow our heart and dreams.

When you are not intentional, there are excuses. When you are not intentional, there is someone to blame. When you are not intentional, you wonder "what happened?" When you are not intentional, you look for someone else to do something. When you are not intentional, "now" is never the right time to get started. "*Good Intentions*" are not enough. To be intentional, you've got to do something. A story helped me understand this principle:

There was a certain man on a business trip who was staying downtown at a hotel. One morning on his way to a meeting, while walking he came upon a young man at a shoe shine stand. As he was approaching the young man, he heard him counting out loud, *"98, 99, 100 ... Good Morning Sir, you can be my 100th customer this week.*

Today is my birthday and in celebration of it, I am offering my 100th customer a discount on a supreme shoe shine for only $3. The regular price is $5." The man took the offer and allowed the young man to shine his shoes. When was finished, the young man did such a great job that the man gave him an extra $5 tip because it was his birthday. As the man stepped down and began to walk away, he heard ... "98, 99, 100."

A person who is intentional, is not only creative, he also knows what he or she wants. Moreover, if they know what they want but can't find what they need, they will create what they need to get what they want. *"Want comes in conversation, expectation comes in behavior." Les Brown*

> In the same way, faith by itself
> if it is not accompanied by action, is dead
> James 2:17

To be intentional you must *"give up to go up."*

Is there something else you should be doing right now? If so, you're in good company. We all find ourselves distracted from meeting more long-term goals by doing more enjoyable short-term activities. Why is it so difficult to stay the course on our long-term projects, even when we are certain that the advantages of sticking to it will far outweigh the more immediate benefits of putting them off? The answer is "instant gratification" the temptation and resulting tendency to forego a future benefit in order to obtain a less rewarding but more immediate benefit.

It's a natural human urge to want good things and to want them NOW. There's nothing wrong with planning for the future, but actions that are taken to benefit you in the here and now are much more advantageous than having to wait a while for them. We know what we want and we want it NOW. The flip side of instant gratification is delayed gratification, or the decision to put off satisfying your desire in order to gain an even better reward or benefit in the future. It's easy to see how delayed gratification is generally the wiser behavior, but we still struggle on a daily basis with the temptation to give in to our immediate desires.

For those of us who are parents, this commitment to make sacrifices for our children's future comes naturally. We will make the sacrifice and not have for ourselves to ensure that our children get what they need. For me, my instant gratification was fulfilling a childhood dream of owning a motorcycle. I had owned one previously but no longer had it. I love riding and wanted another one, so I had saved for 3 years to purchase this new bike. In 2017, in my pursuit and need to grow, and improve self, I realized I needed to put into practice what I had come to know as the Law of Sacrifice by Napoleon Hill:

Be willing to let go of something of Lesser Value
for the attainment of something of a Higher Value.

I made up my mind to invest in myself and my future instead of something that would give me great pleasure in the here and now. I took the money that I had saved and went through a certification program to become a speaker, trainer, and coach specializing in leadership development. This decision has paid off for me many times over as I have since been able to help others to discover their hidden potential and to reach their individual goals.

WORK HARDER ON YOURSELF THAN ON YOUR JOB

LIFE

When You Are Casual About Life
You Will End Up A Casualty.

4

EMBRACE YOUR DESTINY

When one is intentional, he or she discovers purpose. When one knows and understands what they are supposed to do, they pursue it.

Destiny drives purpose, while purpose drives action

Many people want to experience their destiny from God, yet they are not willing to embrace the path to get there. Have you ever asked yourself the question, *"what is the purpose of achieving a goal?"* Many would respond with "ultimately obtaining what you had set out to do." Once you have obtained what you were after, then what? You set another goal, right? I have learned that the purpose is not the goal itself, but the process you had to go through to get there. In other words, it's the journey, not the destination. *It's what you have become to get where you are.*

> You will keep on guiding me with Your counsel
> leading me to a glorious destiny
> Psalm 73:24

We must understand that what God calls us to is so important, that we first must be prepared for it. He's not going to hand us something where we have no idea how to walk in it. He's not going to entrust us with something until we have the maturity to handle it. So, as we embrace our destiny, we must embrace God's preparation process as well. This is where it breaks down for most people. They want the result without the process. We must embrace the path of maturity to experience our destiny.

**"Everything you are going through
is preparing you for what you asked for."**

To Embrace Your Destiny ... <u>You Need to Ask God Some Questions</u>

In order for me to see myself as God saw me and to find out what His plans were for my life, I had to ask Him some important questions:

What do You want to do in my life? What do You want to do through my life? What do You still desire for me to experience? What possibilities lie within me? What potential lies before me? What could I become? What did You have in mind for me when I was created? What do You desire for me? These questions only God can answer. God has placed within you more than you realize.

**"What lies behind us, and what lies before us are
but tiny matters compared to what lies within us."
Ralph Waldo Emerson**

To Embrace Your Destiny ... You Must Go Through the Fire

Each day is a new day. Where I am now has resulted from where I have been. James 1:2-4 *"…whenever trouble comes your way, let it be an opportunity for joy. For when your faith is tested, your endurance has a chance to grow. So, let it grow, for when your endurance is fully developed, you will be strong in character and ready for anything."* (NLT)

Trials in this life are opportunities for us to grow, develop, and mature. Our response to these events determines whether we grow or not. Not all trials produce good results. Not all trials produce maturity. That depends entirely on us!

> That the trail of your faith, being much more precious
> than of gold that perisheth, though it be tried by fire,
> might be found unto praise and honor and
> glory at the appearing of Jesus Christ.
> 1 Peter 1"7

To Embrace Your Destiny ... Know There's Something in The Struggle

So many people in life want everything without any effort. Many want what others have but are unwilling to do what it takes to get it. Many believers have the attitude that because they are saved and in the family of God, that God should give them everything they ever dreamed of without effort, work, or discipline on their part. God wants you to prosper and be blessed, but you must earn it.

There is a struggle and there is a fight you must face. To be what God has ordained you to be, a struggle is necessary.

In Numbers 13:25-33, we see that God left giants in the land for a purpose. Following are some of the lessons I learned from the children of Israel while in the wilderness:

How to fight.

> The weapons of our warfare are mighty through
> the pulling down of strongholds
> 2 Corinthians 4:3-4

Giants or challenging problems help to distinguish between professors and possessors. It's one thing to confess the promises of God. It's another thing to strap on your sword, face your giants, and possess your promises. In other words, what did God say concerning my situation?

> Taking the sword of the Spirit
> which is the Word of God.
> Ephesians 6:14

Giants expose the grasshoppers in the crowd. When giants show up, grasshoppers speak up. Grasshoppers usually blend into the environment, but giants uncover them. Remember, grasshoppers don't eat grapes. You can be so close to experiencing the fullness of

God's blessing for your life but if you don't believe it's for you, it will not happen.

**You will never have promised land faith
with a grasshopper mentality.**

<u>You get to know yourself in the struggle</u> (the real you is discovered under pressure)

<u>You get to know God in the struggle</u> (you realize that God is your only help)

<u>The struggle produces thankfulness.</u> When you know you have to fight for what you get, you appreciate it more and won't let anyone take it from you.

<u>The struggle will test your level of commitment.</u> The only way to truly gauge your level of commitment is when things get hard and challenging.

<u>The struggle qualifies you for rest.</u>

Come unto me, all ye that labor and are heavy laden
and I will give you rest
Matthew 11:28

<u>The struggle qualifies you for the reward.</u> Understand that many times the struggle, the fight, the warfare, the praying, the waiting patiently,

the enduring, is as important as the blessing or reward. While we are looking at the reward, God is looking at the development that is taking place through the struggle, the building of character that is important in all aspects of life.

"Knowing this, that the trying of your faith worketh patience."
James 1:3

My wife, Yolanda, loves butterflies. The caterpillar goes through a process of metamorphosis through which changes from an earthbound crawly worm form into a beautiful butterfly. But this process involves struggle. To cut the struggle short would rob the butterfly of its destiny.

Here is the best thing about the struggle. ___It qualifies you to help others.___ When you have been through something, you can help somebody else. When you have stood your ground and fought your battles and conquered your giants, you are qualified to help someone else through their battles. What God shared with me is that many people can be helped and encouraged as a result of me going through what I have gone through. It is the sharing of our testimonies with others of God's faithfulness to fulfill His promises in our lives that encourages others to *"look unto the hills which will come their help."*

It's our moments of struggle that define us.
How we handle them is what matters.

To Embrace Your Destiny ... <u>*You Must Practice Biblical Principles*</u>

One of my goals in life is to be an Agent of Change, that my life shall be one of significance. In John 10:10 Jesus said, ***"I have come that ye may have life, and that ye may have it more abundantly."*** The ultimate purpose of Jesus coming to this world was to redeem us back to God by paying the price for our sins on Calvary. By doing this, He also made it possible that we could make an impact on the world by our obedience to the will of the Father.

> Let your light so shine before men that they
> may see your good works and glorify
> your Father which is in heaven.
> Matthew 5:16

We can make a difference in the lives of others. Do you want to truly make a difference? Do you want to live a life that Jesus came for you to have? Do you want to live your life purposefully? Are you willing to make the commitment necessary? If so, embrace this principle, it will help you:

Without Change, There Is No Growth.

This truth has changed my life and helped me see and understand clearly what my purpose in life is now and has placed me on a path of living a life that matters.

Back in 2012, I came to discover that *"your purpose can change during different seasons of life."* For 23 years, life had meaning and purpose as I worked in ministry helping the homeless at the Open-Door Rescue Mission. After this season of my life was over, however, I asked God, "now what?" Feeling deep down that there was more He wanted from me, I was given a vision that I would be used in a capacity that would reach far beyond my imagination. I had no idea that it would apply to so many areas of my life. Little did I know that even now, as I have approached a new season in my life, my purpose is being redefined even more. In order for a dream to take on belief one must:

Narrow one's focus on one idea.
This will give birth to other opportunities.

The one idea was that I needed to work on myself. I realized that I needed to **First Add Value to Myself, Then I Would Be Equipped to Help Others.** Consider this:

And Jesus increased in wisdom and stature
and in favor with God and man.
Luke 2:52

This passage in essence says Jesus grew ("increased"). He evolved; he did not stay the same. He changed. Change is sometimes difficult for many people because they don't like being outside of their comfort zone. They like it safe and familiar. Put another way:

"Not everything that is faced can be changed
but nothing can be changed until it is faced."
Novelist James Baldwin

There must be a willingness for change. To grow you must be willing to let your present and future be unlike your past. Your history is not your destiny.

There are four areas of human development we see in the life of Jesus that every person ought to give attention. They are intellectual, physical, social, and spiritual. On this journey there were two areas in particular that I needed to work on. First, it was my <u>Intellectual Development</u>:

The Bible places considerable emphasis upon the development of the mind. Romans 12: 2 says, ***"And be not conformed to this world but be ye transformed by the renewing of your mind, that ye may know what is the good and acceptable, and perfect will of God."***

Finally, brethren, whatsoever things are true, honest, just,
pure, of good report; if there be any virtue,
and any praise, think on these things.
Philippians 4:8

What thoughts do we allow into our minds? Consider the sources: messages on television, social media, and even the opinions of people. Do these thoughts build you up or tear you down? Do they support your goals and dreams? What fears are you struggling with that have captured your thoughts in believing that "it's not possible"? Think about it.

> Casting down imaginations and every high thing that exalted
> itself against the knowledge of God, and bringing into
> captivity every thought to the
> obedience of Christ.
> 2 Corinthians 10:5

It is important to know that God wants us to grow intellectually. **Knowledge is good, however without "knowing Christ" it is useless.** To be worth anything it must lead to a changed life and rightful living. Unfortunately, the truth is that many people want help with their situation, but they don't want to read the Bible or any other books to learn of ways to improve their situation.

> *For this cause we also, since the day we heard it, do not*
> *cease to pray for you and to desire that ye might be*
> *filled with the knowledge of his will in all*
> *wisdom and spiritual understanding.*
> *Colossians 1:9*

> *The heart of the prudent getteth knowledge*
> *and the ear of the wise seeketh knowledge.*
> *Proverbs 18:15*

> *The fear of the LORD is the beginning of knowledge:*

but fools despise wisdom and instruction
Proverbs 1:7

For me as a Man of Faith who loves and believes in the Word of God, in order to reach others, I had to be able to identify with them. We must know and understand where they come from intellectually. We must expose ourselves to different concepts and matters to gain understanding. We must be able to go where they are in order to get them where God wants them to be. The Apostle Paul said in 1 Corinthians 9:22:

> To the weak became I as weak, that I might gain
> the weak: I am made all things to all men, that I
> might by all means save some.

Paul became all things to all men as a goal in reaching some for Christ. He, like Jesus, adapted his teaching to their culture and experiences in order to reach them. We should never change the message but may have to change the method in order to be relevant today to those who would receive the hope we have.

In January of 2016, I made a personal commitment to begin reading books to broaden my knowledge base on different subject matters and to be able to better identify with people. One thing I discovered is that if you want people to be impressed with you, share your successes, but if you want people to identify with you, talk about your mistakes. It does not matter who you are or where you come from, we all have one thing in common. All of us are sinners.

For all have sinned and come short of the glory of God.

Romans 3:26

This is where we can connect with people. We are no different from them. God found us all at a place of hopelessness, brokenness, and despair, but because of his love toward us, *while we were yet sinners, Christ died.*

Secondly it was my Spiritual Development: Clearly, the most neglected dimension of human development is spiritual growth. ***"Faith cometh by hearing and hearing by the Word of God." (Romans 10:17)***

Because God is spirit and we are created in His image, our relationship with Him must be at a spiritual level. Growing in the grace and knowledge of our Lord Jesus Christ is required and absolutely vital to all who have accepted Jesus as their Savior. Babies do not remain as such. They grow, and so should we.

As newborn babes, desire the sincere
milk of the word that ye
may grow thereby.
1 Peter 2:2

I found that I needed to spend more time with God. In *God's Purpose for My Pain* (the chapter "Strength Renewed"), I wrote of the time when God revealed to me that nothing should be more important, not even my relationship with my wife, than my relationship and fellowship with Him. When you spend adequate time with God you are equipped with what it takes to please Him. Psalm 119:11 says ***"Thy word have I hid in my heart that I might not sin against thee."*** How much time do you spend with God alone in prayer and reading his word daily? Is the first time you've opened your bible all week on Sunday Morning at worship service?

We often have a tendency to be selfish and self-centered. However, to be a person of significance, you must put others first. You put others first by getting to know them, their interest, concerns, needs, and dreams. "No man is an island." People need people. Zig Ziglar once said, *"If you first help others get what they want, they will help you get what you want."* This is what motivated me to want to help others reach their full God-given potential in all areas of life.

If you have ever flown on an airplane, you are familiar with the pre-flight instructions given by the flight attendants that state *"in the event of an emergency you must first put on your oxygen mask before helping others."* You must take the time necessary to make sure that you are constantly growing, learning, and adding value to yourself that you might be all that you can be for Christ and others.

To Embrace Your Destiny … <u>*You Must Cooperate with God*</u>

To cooperate with God is to first have that intimacy with Him that is so close that He can communicate with you what His will is for you. Did not Jesus say in John 10:27, ***"My sheep know my voice."***

Secondly, you will discover purpose and begin living out that purpose through Jesus.

I can do all things through Christ who strengthen me
Philippians 4:19

This requires taking risks and doing things you have never done before. Putting off the old self, and eagerly picking up new skills that enable you to explore the undiscovered talents within.

In 2017, I began Destiny Development Design, a 501© 3 non-profit ministry. In 2020, I began J.G. Farris Consulting, a consulting business that is a Christian company. Both organizations help individuals grow in reaching their full potential personally, professionally, and spiritually. These results are accomplished by using biblical and universal principles through multiple formats of speaking engagements, workshops, and trainings in evangelism, personal growth, leadership development and youth enrichment.

I now found myself totally outside of my comfort zone. Sure, I served as the executive director of the Open-Door Rescue Mission for 23 years, but it had been established since 1949. This venture was totally from the ground up, and if it was to be successful, I would need God's help. I felt God's lead in that I was within my passion and skill set of speaking and teaching. They would be vehicles in which I could "reach beyond the walls" of the church, not only into the corporate sector but also into schools with the Good News of Jesus Christ.

To become something, you've never been you must do something you've never done.
Les Brown

In December 2017, I stepped out in faith and scheduled my first training workshop on principles of leadership. For over 26 years, I grew confident in God and my abilities to facilitate and teach on material I was familiar with, namely God's Word. However, at that moment I honestly experienced great anxiety because I had never done this before. To lessen this feeling, I would often read the following quote by an unknown author entitled "Uncommon Man":

"I do not choose to be a common man. It is my right to be uncommon — if I can. I seek opportunity — not security. I do not wish to be a kept citizen, humbled and dulled by having the state look after me. I want to take the calculated risk; to dream and to build, to fail and to succeed. I refuse to barter incentive for a dole. I prefer the challenges of life to the guaranteed existence; the thrill of fulfillment to the stale calm of utopia. I will not trade freedom for beneficence nor my dignity for a handout. I will never cower before any master nor bend to any threat. It is my heritage to stand erect, proud and unafraid; to think and act for myself, enjoy the benefit of my creations, and to face the world boldly and say, ***this I have done."***

The enemy, Satan, does not want us to be successful because he knows God will get glory. Fear is a tool he uses to paralyze and keep us from stepping out in faith, trusting that God will be there and do what He says He will do. I call this fear *"FALSE EVIDENCE APPEARING REAL."*

There was a story of a young man who had recently landed a new job and moved into a new neighborhood. His next-door neighbor, whose property was fenced in, had a dog that would every morning come out viciously at the young man as he walked by to catch the bus. Thank God for the fence. On one particular day, as normal, the dog came out. Unfortunately, someone left the gate unlocked and the dog began chasing the young man. Knowing he could not out run the dog, the young man stopped, picked up a stick, and turned around to hit the dog. He noticed when the dog was upon him that it had no teeth.

What are you fearful of that has no teeth? Is it the fear of failure? The fear of trading security for the unknown? The fear of what others will think about you? The fear of success? Do you know that 85% of people will allow the fear of failure to outweigh their desire to succeed? Remember no teeth.

God did not give us a spirit of fear
but of love, power, and a sound mind
2 Timothy 1:7

**You can have more than you've got because
you can become more than you are.**

LIFE

*Life at its best is a life
surrendered to Jesus Christ.*
Pastor Charles Stanley

5

LIVING BY DESIGN

Living by Design is ...
Destiny Communicated to Us by God.

I emphasize, "to us by God." It is God who initiates our destiny. It is not and was not ever our idea. Just because you've always wanted to do or be something does not mean that is "your destiny." It may have been a dream or goal.

Spending summers in Alabama as a child with my grandparents, I dreamed of becoming a Greyhound Bus driver. This dream came from sitting on the front seat of the bus next to the driver every trip back and forth visiting. The love for driving, the open road, and traveling across the country is still with me so much that when I became an adult, I purchased a motorcycle. But guess what, I never became a Greyhound Bus driver. Nothing wrong with the idea, but that was not to be my destiny. I'm sure you too had childhood dreams that did not come true.

A Biblical example could be seen in the life of Moses who was raised in Egypt for 40 years. He had the education and resources needed to deliver the people out of the hands of Pharaoh then, but that was neither the right time nor what God had in mind on how His people would be set free. Moses had some wilderness training that he would have to go through first to prepare him for what God had in mind. Once training was over, God spoke directly to Moses of what his destiny and purpose would be.

"My thoughts are not your thoughts
neither are my ways your ways
saith the Lord."
Isaiah 55:8

The same was true for me. Over the years I had to go through some wilderness training that was necessary in preparing me for what God had in store for me. God has spoken me concerning over three and a half decades of ministry.

His lord said to him, 'Well done, good and faithful servant
you have been faithful over a few things
I will make you ruler over many things.
Enter into the joy of your lord.'
Matthew 25:23

When one is faithful and a good steward with what he or she has been given, God rewards them with more. I patiently wait with anticipation on just what that will be for I believe God is not done with me yet.

Living by Design is …
Destiny that is for the Blessing of a Larger Focus.

One day God spoke to me about a ministry that would *"reach beyond these walls,"* beyond the traditional Sunday morning worship experience within a church congregational setting. This was to be done on a daily basis with people outside of the church where I currently served.

It was to reach as many people as possible on a consistent basis. Generally, those of us who do attend worship weekly will receive a word at least once, maybe twice a week. Let me remind you just in case it has been a while:

> Not forsaking the assembling of ourselves together,
> as the manner of some is but exhorting one
> another: and so much the more
> as ye see the day approaching.
> Hebrews 10:25

There are many remarkable ministries that God is using to strengthen the Body of Christ and bring the lost to himself, but nothing is as vital and important in the life and development of the believer as the local church. It is the coming together of the saints where faith is seen up close in person.

There are those, however, who do not go to church, let alone receive a word of hope from God's word. I was burdened within my spirit to make a way that the average believer could minister to their friends and family, thus fulfilling the mandate of the Great Commission. I initially thought God wanted me to prepare a brief word and delegate someone else to send it out. But God told me He did not give that for someone else to do. He gave it for me to do. I was obedient to God, and this became the birth of a ministry that is now in its 10th year. It's called *"Grow Your Faith Today – The GYFT Podcast."*

I asked God the question, how? He had me look in Exodus chapter 14 at Moses and what he was told to do when Pharaoh was behind him and the children of Israel with mountains on both sides and the Red Sea before him. What Moses had in his hand was all he needed to deliver God's people. It was a rod that he stretched forth over the sea and divided it. For me, it would be a cell phone. God showed me how important it is to use what you have. Please realize that what you have is enough to accomplish what is needed with focus and faith in God.

Grow Your Faith Today is a daily ministry of inspiration and encouragement in an audio text format. What started out to an audience of just 72 people of family and close friends locally has since grown to hundreds, if not thousands of people. Frankly I am not sure how many, and it really is not important for me to the point where I think more of myself than the purpose.

Therefore, in order to keep me from becoming conceited

> I was given a thorn in my flesh, a messenger
> of Satan to torment me
> 2 Corinthians 12:7

It is sent all over the nation and has reached 21 other countries. What makes it unique is the partnership of believers simply sharing the message of hope with other people they know.

I say this not to brag on myself but on my God. I have a beloved brother in the Lord who lives in Louisiana who shares the GYFT Podcast with daily sending to over 360 people. Since 2017, of those whom he consistently witnesses to, a countless number of people have come to accept Jesus Christ as Savior. I am grateful to God for him in using this as an extension of his ministry.

> I have planted, Apollos watered; but God give the increase.
> 1 Corinthians 3:6

Another young minister, who lives in Mississippi, shares with 9 co-workers at work as part of their daily devotional time. There is a sister in Las Vegas, who, if I am delayed in sending the devotional as scheduled, will not hesitate to text me letting me know she didn't get her word today. And there are countless other partners I am blessed to be a co-laborer with as part of this ministry. All I can say is …

BUT GOD!

Not by power, nor by might but by my spirit saith the Lord
Zechariah 4:6-8

In my book, *God's Purpose for My Pain*, *God told me "You will meet some people who will bless you, and will touch lives far beyond your comprehension."* God is just AWESOME!

This is bigger than you and me. This is about transformation and increasing the scope of effectiveness for God. God always has a larger plan He wants fulfilled. He calls individuals, but His plans affect the masses.

My goal is to prepare God's people for Kingdom Purposes. Kingdom Purpose goes far beyond our local church. Kingdom Purpose is to do the work of the ministry (Ephesians 4:2), to equip the believer to win souls for Jesus Christ. (Matthew 28:19-20) To apply the Gospel to every situation at hand, wherever "at hand or along the way" may be.

Did not Jesus say … ***"Greater works will you do."***

Living by Design is …
Destiny that Open Doors of Opportunity

A man's gift will make room for him
and bring him before great men.
Proverbs 18:16

I now understand that this verse has nothing to do with physical gifts. Rather, it speaks of the gift you carry inside. Your unique talent or ability. The thing you do better than most people, almost without effort. You know, that thing when you do it, people commend you and ask for more. That thing you do which comes easy to you, and yet, blesses others … that's your gift. Everybody has a gift. It was given to you by God. Unfortunately, not everybody develops their gift. Pablo Picasso, the famous painter, once said, *"The meaning of life is to find your gift. The purpose of life is to give it away."*

A great example is the story of Joseph in the Old Testament. Most of you remember the story. He was imprisoned for a crime he didn't commit. While in jail, he met Pharaoh's chief butler. The butler had a dream, and Joseph interpreted it correctly in telling him he would be reinstated in Pharaoh's service – and he was. One day Pharaoh also had a dream that nobody was able to interpret. The dream was that a great famine would come upon the land. That's when the butler remembered Joseph.

Joseph was brought before Pharaoh. And the rest, as they say, is history. Joseph went on to become prime minister in Egypt – second only to Pharaoh. His gift made room for him and brought him before Pharaoh.

In October of 2014, I got a job working for an automotive parts plant as a machine operator. It became one of those situations I found contentment in and was thankful for because it paid the bills; however, *it was not a career move.* One day I was talking to the

Environmental Health and Safety Manager and shared with him that I was a consultant and that I did trainings in leadership development and personal growth. He mentioned this to the newly hired plant manager who was looking to make some positive changes in the plant. We met, and I was able to share with him firsthand of what I had observed working there for 4 years.

He was so impressed with my professionalism and written assessment of the conditions of the plant that he allowed me to make a proposal to him for some needed training. I found favor with him and was allowed to provide four 8-week, 90-minute workshops at 6:00 a.m. before my regular work shift. I taught a class in personal growth for both hourly and management employees. And yes, praise God I was appropriately compensated for this service provided.

BUT GOD!

"When you know your worth,
you will stop giving people discounts."
Chinese Proverb

Mind you, previously, to my employer I had been just an ordinary machine operator that could be replaced by anyone in the blink of an eye to do the job. On one occasion when I met with the plant superintendent in determining what his needs may be for his supervisors and line leaders, he was astonished and asked me the question. "Knowing what you know, why are you here?" My reply was that I was on assignment from God and that:

A man's gift will make room for him
and bring him before great men.
Proverbs 18:16

He shook his head in amazement and asked me where that quote was from. I smiled. The bottom line for a child of God is this: doors of opportunities will open because <u>*God does not call the qualified. He qualifies the called.*</u>

**Don't set your goals in regards to your abilities
set your goals in regards to the God you serve.**

LABOR

Life is like a Camera

Focus on what's important

Capture the good times

Develop from the negatives

And if things don't work

out Take another shot.

6

DON'T WASTE YOUR VALLEYS

Beautiful things can grow in a valley

As with me, you may have experienced many valleys in life. Valleys can be considered self-inflicting (the consequences of bad choices made, maybe even called sin) or God-prescribed (divinely arranged with a purpose in mind as in the story of Job). All valleys, whether self-inflicted or by God, include suffering, low moments of frustration, anxiety, regrets, disappointments, and have within them valuable lessons that are to be extracted and applied to our lives to make us better.

> **Life is not the way it is supposed to be.**
> **It is the way it is. The way you cope with it**
> **is what makes the difference.**
> **Virginia Satir**

How you see your valley has everything to do with your attitude about your valley. We often see a valley as something negative and as something we would rather avoid. But valleys are part of the journey called life.

Life has a tendency to be unfair, and hurt can come due to loss, but what is so amazing about God is that He is still there for us. He's there to forgive, heal, and help us. He is faithful, for He said, **"I will never leave you nor forsake you."** It is because of His faithfulness, God wants to get glory in all things, even our valleys.

He wants to show Himself mighty in situations where the only way relief, miracles, or breakthroughs can happen is that He provides it and that there is no question about how we got where we are.

In Isaiah 61, God spoke through the prophet Isaiah to the people of Israel that even though they were experiencing suffering, loss, and pain, (their valley) due to choices they made, hope was still present and that He would be merciful to them. He gave them hope in the midst of their situation.

He wants us to give all of our cares, problems, failures - our "ashes" to Him. He will exchange those ashes and give us beauty. Many people want God to take care of them, but they continue worrying or trying to figure out the answers to their problems instead of waiting for His directions. They continue to wallow in their "ashes" and expect Him to give them beauty. But understand, it doesn't work that way. He will give you beauty but only after you give Him your ashes.

Even in the midst of our valleys, we have hope because, 1) its temporary, *"ye though I walk through the valley of the shadow of death*.... and 2) we are not alone, *"I will fear no evil for thou art with me"* *(Psalm 23).* The valley was not designed for you to stay there.

Success meets you where you step, not where you stand

Following are some beautiful things I found in the valley:

Every next level of life is going to require a Next Level You.

If you always keep doing what you have done you will always get what you always have had.
Les Brown

Valleys are opportune times in life to not only see where you are and how you got there but also to see them as opportunities to learn, grow, and become better. You can only be responsible for you.

In 2012, I experienced a new me. I held within me bitterness, envy, and pride, all sins that I knew did not please God. My heart had been broken due to some disappointments, misunderstandings, and misfortunes. Sin will take you where you don't want to go and keep you longer than you want to stay. It will hold back the windows of heaven from being opened in your life. It was not until I confessed my sins (not that of others) before God that I received his forgiveness.

If we confess our sins, he is faithful and just to forgive us our sins
and to cleanse us from all
unrighteousness.
1 John 1:9

BUT GOD!

What accompanied this forgiveness from God was that He even
made my enemies be at peace with me. He brought financial relief
to a situation that I personally caused and restored back to me what
the enemy had taken.

Every round goes higher and higher

In November 2012, my mother, Levolia, passed and went home to
be with the Lord. Needless to say, this was a valley in my life, for she
was my first love. If ever the Word of God was real in my life, this
was another time that I witnessed its power. Having lost Helene three
years prior gave me reassurance that I would be able to face this time
in my life as well.

I had mentioned in the introduction of my first book that *"of all
the grief counseling I have done over 19 years of pastoral ministry, no
experience has ever taken me to a level so devastating as this one that
began on August 5, 2009, at 8:53 am. How thankful I was to God that
when it comes to having lost a loved one, I will be able to share with
others just what God can do."* [1]

That level of grace and comfort from God was experienced at a time in my life when I lost my wife and didn't know how I was going to make it. Now I needed another level of grace, for this was my mother, and again God proved himself faithful. The difference was now my faith in God was stronger. It was with that strength and confidence that I was able to preach my mother's eulogy and give comfort to others.

It is once more that I would need God's grace for grief had visited my family once again. On August 27, 2020, my youngest son, Dion, passed and went home to be with the Lord. Son, I love you and miss you tremendously.

BUT GOD!

> Who comforted us in all our tribulation, that we may be able
> to comfort them which are in any trouble, by the
> comfort wherewith we ourselves are
> comforted of God
> 2 Thessalonians 1:4

Death is a part of life and God always has purpose for the pain we experience. Even though it is a "low" moment in all our lives and one in which none of us can avoid, knowing God and His promises to those who have died in the Lord can be our motivation to share with others the salvation and hope we have in the Good News of Jesus Christ.

Then I heard a voice from heaven say, "Write this:
Blessed are the dead who die in the LORD from now on
Yes," says the Spirit, "they will rest from their labor
for their deeds will follow them.
Revelations 14:13

Sometimes You Win, Sometimes You Learn [2]

One factor that has contributed to my growth in these 14 years is what I have learned, not what I have lost. There are things we can learn when we have experienced loss, failure or "find ourselves in a valley." When you are losing, it seems like everything hurts. When I speak of loss it could refer to the death of a loved one, health issues, loss of income, divorce, a demotion on the job, setbacks, being emotionally stuck, or mentally defeated. For some, these can affect their identity because they will wear it as a badge of dishonor. It can cause one not only to feel like they have failed but also that they are a failure. But understand, failure is not a bad thing. It is a part of the process of becoming successful. Failure is a way of learning.

FAILURE IS NOT FINAL

Nothing in life is worthwhile unless you take risks. Nelson Mandela once said ***"There is no passion to be found in life playing small and settling for a life that is less than what you are capable of living."*** Give it all you got, and when you fail, because you will fail in life, always fall forward not backward.

Another name for failure can be "education." Some people may think that it is experience that is the best teacher in life.

Experience in and of itself is not the best teacher
but it sure does serve as the best excuse
for not trying to do the
same silly thing again.
Frank Hughes

We can go through something over and over again, not learn from it, and continue making the same mistakes. Why? Because we did not step back and reflect on what just happened. It is the *evaluated experience* that is the best teacher. It is taking your mistakes, failures, disappointments, and loss of all types, and properly gleaning from them the positive lessons that can take you to the next level. In essence, it is changing some things from what was.

Let's face it, life is unfair at times. Things do not always work as we want. **Ten percent of life is what happens, ninety percent is how we respond.** What do you do when things don't work out as you would like? What do you do when you have prayed to God for something and He says "no"? How did those who found success get there? It was not that they did not fail, but that they used their failures as motivation to press on. They accepted what happened and learned from it what to do differently. They did not allow their mistakes to paralyze them or allow multiple setbacks to keep them from trying again.

Then there will be those who will not try at all because the "time is not right." If not now, when? If not you, then who? They will convince themselves to wait. There is virtue in waiting but not if waiting is due to the fear of failing. Fear is not of God. (2 Timothy 1:7)

Some may wait because they simply don't feel like doing anything right now. They need someone or something to motivate them. I get it, encouragement is important, but let me remind you that there are times when there will be no one to encourage you. It is at those times that you need to man up, woman up, hold your head up, and like David, encourage yourself. (1 Samuel 30:6)

One thing that I've been able to do is take ownership of failures I have made. I have failed in many areas of my life. Looking back now, there are some things I should have done differently. I have some regrets in the raising of my sons, my ministry, and with my love, Yolanda. I've made some unwise, selfish choices that I paid for, but through it all I've learned from them. Thank God for his mercies.

A loss is a total loss ONLY if you learn nothing from it.

In everything there is a lesson to be learned. The question is, how do we find a way of learning from our losses? Again, the key is to again be intentional, have the right attitude, and see it from God's perspective. There is something God has purposed in the situation and it is designed to eventually be for your good. Failure is part of the process of becoming successful.

> For we know that all things work together for the good
> to them who love the God, to them who are the
> called according to his purpose.
> Romans 8:28

We find lessons from losing through …

Humility, for it is the Spirit of Learning. [3]
Pride is not thinking too much about yourself but thinking about yourself too much.

Pride goeth before destruction, and a haughty spirit before a fall.
Proverb 16:18

We find lessons from losing through …

Improvement, for it is the Focus of Learning. [4]
Losses are confirmation that improvement is needed. What you want must first begin in you.

If you want a friend, you must first "work on" being friendly. If you want a good spouse, you must first "work on" being a good spouse. If you want things to be better, you must first "work on" becoming a better you. If you want a greater quality of life, you must first "work on" improving your skill set. You can be more efficient, reach your full potential, and greater opportunities will open up for you, but the key is it starts with "You" becoming better first.

BE THAT CHANGE YOU WANT TO SEE IN OTHERS

<u>We find lessons from losing through ...</u>

Adversity, for it is the Catalyst of Learning. [5]
Each one of us can relate to events in our lives that have shocked the very foundation of our being and have caused great pain. However, it is how we respond that will make the difference.

We can respond like a carrot in boiling water that goes soft, having a "Woe is me" attitude. We can respond like an egg in boiling water that becomes hard on the inside. This response to adversity is one of denial, not facing what has happened, let alone what needs to be done to change for the better. Or, we can respond like the coffee bean in hot water, intentionally making everything around us better in the midst of the situation. In other words, we can make something good come out of a bad situation.

When times are trying, that is not the time to stop trying.

Notes
1. See the author's book, *God's Purpose for My Pain* (ASA Publishing 2010, page 7)
2. John C. Maxwell, Sometimes You Win Sometimes You Learn (Hachette Book Group 2015)

3. Ibid
4. Ibid
5. Ibid

LABOR

If you spend one hour daily in your field
for 5 years, you will be an
expert in that field
Jim Rohn

7

THERE'S POWER IN THE TONGUE

We become what we repeatedly do – Aristotle

The things you do on a daily basis will help shape your future. One thing I have done in my personal development is establish and maintain a daily routine of self-discipline. I am an early riser and believe that old saying "the early bird catches the worm."

The bigger the dream the earlier you'll get up.
Eric Thomas

My routine will consist of getting up at 4:15 a.m., making a cup of coffee, which I drink only half of, recording and sending out my daily *GYFT* Podcast devotional to ministry partners, having my personal time in devotion, and finally, something that has proven to be a tremendous blessing. It is journaling, specifically my daily prayer journal.

For about four years now, I have daily maintained this journal of prayer, praise, supplications, gratitude to God for prayers answered, needs, concerns, and everything in between for family, friends, acquaintances, neighbors, co-workers, church members, and whosoever needed prayer.

Is anyone among you sick?......
The prayer of a righteous person is powerful and effective
James 5:14-16

I urge, then, first of all, that petitions, prayers
intercession and thanksgiving be made for all people
1 Timothy 2:1

People will share with me in passing about themselves, a loved one, or someone who they know needs prayer. That need will be included in my journal at some time. I'm not bragging but praising God that He has given me this sensitivity of intercession for others and their needs. I have been truly blessed in developing a listening ear to the needs of others and have daily included that in this journal. It is verbally read and revised daily as I have witnessed God moving by His spirit in people's lives, fulfilling their needs, and answering their prayers. I have been able to (through discipline, *being intentional* and strategically) go to the throne of God in prayer on behalf of others.

As I writing, I have been reflecting on how God has been at work in my life lately. One of my priorities is praying for my family, particularly my surviving son Eugene and my grandchildren. Even though Dion is no longer with us, he held a special place in my heart because his need was for a special love from his father. He was a young man with Behavioral Health needs, and I always labored in prayer about his mental, psychological, and physical state. Be assured that you have a special place in your heavenly Father's heart as well.

Let us therefore come boldly unto the throne of grace
that we may obtain mercy, and find grace to help in time of need.
Hebrews 4:16

This spiritual discipline of praying for others has helped me simplify my faith. It has allowed me to stay focused and keep my eye on God. By consistently exercising this discipline of prayer by journaling, I am able to see His will for my life more clearly and live the life He desires for me.

The more we practice the disciplines of studying, meditating on God's Word, and prayer, the better we are at them and the stronger we make our faith. God will then show Himself faithful in answering prayers and fulfilling His word in our lives. I highly recommend journaling, even though I know it may not be for everyone.

Proverbs 18:21 says, *"Death and life are in the power of the tongue, and those who love it will eat its fruit."*

Our destiny here on earth is not up to us, whereas our eternal destiny is. The power of the tongue and of prayer does not flow from us; it is not the special words we say or the way we say them. The power of prayer comes from the omnipotent One who hears our prayers and answers them. Prayer places us in contact with God.

We must choose to speak life as we pray. Our prayers are answered according to our faith (Matthew 9:29), and sometimes in spite of the lack of faith. In Acts 12, the church prayed for Peter's release from prison. God answered their prayer, but they did not believe it was him, refusing to open the door when he came knocking. They failed to expect an answer to their prayers. We MUST expect results. It is irrelevant whether or not He chooses to grant our petitions or deny our requests. Whatever the answer to our prayers, the God to whom we pray is the source of the power of prayer. He can and will answer us according to His perfect will and timing.

We all have limitations, but there is one thing we can do that has no boundaries. It is going to God neither doubting nor worrying but *'in prayer and supplications, with thanksgiving, making our request known unto Him. – Philippians 4:6- 8*

It is because of what God has done in my life these past 14 years, that by faith I pray, speak and believe that He is able to do exceedingly abundantly more than I can ask or imagine.

For the LORD God is a sun and shield: the LORD will give grace
and glory no good thing will he withhold
from them that walk uprightly.
Psalm 84:11

LABOR

When you are bigger than your purpose, it is a career. When purpose is bigger than you, it is your calling and ministry

8

I MUST BE DREAMING

*It's a Beautiful Thing When A Career
and A Passion Come Together*

I mentioned earlier that my job working in an automotive parts plant was an assignment from God, a blessing but not a career move. Because I possessed additional marketable skills, I had applied for numerous job opportunities for years at various companies. I invested my efforts in attempting to get re-certified as a computer program developer and discovered this was not what God wanted me to do. Sometimes we go back to what is familiar, not realizing that God has something much greater for us. I believed that, based on my previous years of experience in management and customer service I would secure something soon. Five years had gone by, and nothing. As God will open doors, so will He keep doors shut if that is not His will for you. I wondered why I had not been able to get a job in any of the positions for which I had applied.

What moves and motivates a person to give it their all and do their best every time? What gets you up in the morning looking forward to doing what you love to do? What will bring the greatest impact and make a difference in the lives of others? When a person is so blessed to be able to work in his or her giftedness, they are truly blessed. Whatever you do for a living, as a hobby, or volunteering to help others, do your best, give your all, and do it as unto the Lord.

> "Let your light so shine that men might
> see your good works and glorify
> your Father in heaven
> Matthew 16:13

My passion and gift that I enjoy more than anything is teaching. To educate, equip, and empower others on becoming the best they can be, are abilities I always felt I've had.

As part of my journey of growing and improving my skill set as a speaker and trainer, as mentioned earlier, I became certified as a John Maxwell Team member. This decision opened up many other opportunities of self-awareness, leadership development, attitude awareness, having a proper mindset, living intentionally with purpose, and understanding that failure was essential in becoming successful in life.

> The steps of a good man are ordered by the Lord
> and He delights in his ways.
> Psalm 37:23

I increased my knowledge base by taking classes in how to manage finances, daily listening to motivational messages, and developing a routine of daily growth by exposing myself to different kinds of interests. As a result of this I am now a lifelong learner in pursuing purpose for my life. The Word of God says, ***"ask and it shall be given, seek and ye shall find, knock and the door shall be opened."***

In December of 2018, I visited a local high school with the desire to volunteer working with young people. There was nothing available at the time, but it was suggested that I apply for a part-time position working as a school lunch monitor. I saw this as an opportunity to get my foot in the door and to begin building relationships with students, teachers, and the school system. I got the job working one hour per day, 5 days a week. This assignment was after a full shift working midnights at the plant.

> Never despise these small beginnings
> for the Lord rejoices to see the work begin.
> Zachariah 4:10

I made up my mind that I was going to step out in faith and believe God for something better. When I made the decision to leave the plant in August 2019, I made the choice to stop …

**Downgrading my dream to fit my reality
but upgrade my convictions to match my destiny.**

When I made this move, God immediately provided a temporary assignment at a middle school working with children with special needs. As soon as that job was finished, I was reassigned to another school at the elementary level. I became very attached to the students I served and experienced unbelievable joy knowing I was helping this very important group.

By the grace of God, I established a good rapport within the school district. It was recommended that I apply for an upcoming permanent position at the high school level where I really wanted to be. I embraced what appeared to be God's will for me, interviewed for the job, and received certification as a Paraprofessional. If someone would have said then that I would be doing what I am now doing, I would have said no way. I could not have planned this.

What You Move Towards, Moves Towards You

BUT GOD!

When one is passionate about what he or she does, even the job is not work. I got the job and am now working with some amazing people (some believers), in an environment with young people and doing what I enjoy.

Relationships are being developed with co-workers, students, and families. I have discovered that God has placed me where I am for some greater purpose. Not only do I have opportunity to teach enrichment courses online to youth, but I now have received training as a Respite Care provider for families with children who have autism.

My heart goes out as a parent for I understand to some degree that caring for a child with special needs present additional challenges that go beyond the everyday stresses of being a parent. Dion, was diagnosed with schizoaffective disorder. His death became my motivation to helping families. Even though he lived to be an adult, as parents, his mother and I realized that our life would be a *"life of care for him."*

I realized that when my workday at school was over, the responsibility of care for families was not over. *THIS IS THEIR LIFE.* Me being able to provide some relief and time for themselves is now a ministry to families. I pray that my presence be an example of God's grace. I often speak of how important it is to position yourself to be blessed by God and a blessing to others. God knows what He is doing.

Stop asking God to bless what you are doing.
Do what God has already blessed.

LABOR

Take Pride in How Far You Have Come

Have Faith in How Far You Can Go

9

THERE'S MORE WORK TO BE DONE

I have been blessed in my life in that I have been in the church literally all my life. I accepted Jesus Christ as my savior as a young boy in the south while visiting my grandparents. My early Christian upbringing include going to Sunday School, Morning Worship, afternoon BTU (Baptist Training Union), Evening Service, and Communion (on first Sundays). During my pre-teen years back here in Michigan, I didn't go to church much. It was not until I met and started dating Helene that I got back in the church. You see, her father, a preacher, wouldn't have it; us dating and me not going to church. The seed that had been planted in me earlier in my life was beginning to germinate.

> Train up a child in the way he should go
> and when he is old, he will not depart from it.
> Proverbs 22:16

After high school I got even more involved with the youth ministry and became a youth leader. Entering my mid-twenties, I felt a stronger calling on my life and was ordained as a deacon. I can recall being trained as a missionary by mothers of the church. Some might remember this pledge that ended our weekly Missionary Society meeting every Wednesday evening:

I Pledge ... By daily reading, meditation and communion with my Lord and Savior Jesus Christ, to live an upright Christian life, To practice His teachings in my dealings with my fellow man, to dedicate my talent and give of my time, influence, and means to teaching or spreading the Christian religion at home and abroad, To win souls through personal service for Christ, To encourage and help in the enlistment of young people in the Christian work, And to make my home a center of Christian light and love. To these ends I pledge -- to devote myself and seek divine aid and guidance daily that I might become a living witness and a bright and shining light for my Lord.

As a young adult and married, Helene and I would take food donated weekly to the Open-Door Rescue Mission, and every Wednesday evening my brother, Arthur Willis, and I would teach a bible study to men at SHAR House East, a substance abuse rehab facility. This was the beginning foundation of my service and commitment to God and His people.

It was in April of 1990 that I shared with my pastor, J.H. Johnson, that I was called by God to preach the gospel of Jesus Christ. Soon afterward, I was ordained as a minister and called to pastor. I organized the True Faith Missionary Baptist Church. We met for worship at the Open Door Rescue Mission for a few years. In February 1994, after the passing of Pastor Herbert Rylander, I was asked by the Board of

Directors to become the director of the Open Door Rescue Mission and by the congregation of Open Door Gospel Tabernacle to serve as their pastor.

I am forever grateful to God for the privilege of the opportunity to have served in both capacities for the Lord. We faced many challenges but overcame them by God's grace. I was blessed to serve and minister to many people through the years. I pray that I made an impact on each person in their spiritual walk and prepared them for their own journey in life.

Having now retired from pastoring, I have not lost my burden for the church and for the winning of souls to Jesus Christ. In 2019, I was introduced to a ministry called Evangelism Explosion which really sparked within me the need to be properly trained in sharing my faith with others. After I received training and coaching, God created opportunities to go into churches and facilitate training workshop on how to effectively witness to others.

If there is one area of improvement that the church in general need, it is equipping people to share their faith. A model of this is the advice of the Apostle Paul to a young Timothy as found in 2 Timothy 2:2:

> And the things that thou have heard of me
> among many witnesses, the same commit thou
> to faithful men, who shall be able to teach others also.

The making and equipping of disciples to pass on their faith is the ultimate mandate of the great commission of Jesus to His church. It is not until all believers are telling others of the Good News, and what they have learned, that the kingdom of God here on earth will expand geometrically and began making the impact that God desires.

It's amazing to know that we as believers have all we need to be a witness for the Lord. NO SEMINARY NEEDED. Simply telling your story of what God has meant to you is more than enough. May we do our part in being faithful and leave the results to God.

As we look now over 3 decades later, God has been faithful.

We've come this far by faith, leaning on the Lord.
Trusting in his holy word. He's never failed me yet.
Oh... I can 't turnaround, we've come this far by faith.

The book of Ecclesiastes says "Everything has it's time and season."

To everything there is a season
and a time to every purpose under the heaven
Ecclesiastes 3:1

I am now, as earlier mentioned, in a new season of my life. My desire for my life, my labor (what I do), and my love (my relationships) is that God's will be done, He be pleased, and that He alone gets the glory. A favorite verse that I live by and cling to is Psalm 37:4-5

"Delight yourself in the Lord and He will give you the desires of
your heart. Commit thy ways unto him and
he shall bring it to pass"

By fully understanding the love God has for me as his child, I have
embraced "his desire" as my own. Here is what I mean:

We are first introduced to the word delight in Genesis 22:2 with
Abraham being tested by God to sacrifice his son, Isaac: "**Take your
son, your only son, whom you love—Isaac—and go to the region
of Moriah. Sacrifice him there as a burnt offering on a mountain
I will show you.**"

In Hebrew, the word for love in this passage is the word "Ahab"
which means "to love, to desire, delight." The word "Delight" is
describing a father's love for his child. In doing so, He introduces
his own delighting love for His children, that is for those who have
accepted his son, Jesus Christ, as Savior. He describes the way He
feels about His child; His daughter, Toni, in Florida; son, James in
Nashville; daughter, Chloe, in Michigan; Felicia in California; Yvette,
in Alabama, and yes, you reading this right now.

Notice, that "Delight" has nothing to do with you or me, but
everything to do with "His love for us." This is why nothing can
separate us from that love.

For I am convinced that neither death nor life, neither angels nor
demons, neither the present nor the future, nor any powers,

> neither height nor depth, nor anything else in
> all creation, will be able to separate us
> from the love of God that is in
> Christ Jesus our LORD.
> Romans 8:38-39

See, it's all about Him.

The second important word of that passage is the word "desire." The prefix "de" means "of" and "sire" means "father." Together the word "desire" means "of the Father." I see an Aha moment coming. What God showed me was this:

"Allow the father (God) and His only son (Jesus) that He so delights in to delight in you (Jerome) in that same way, and when that happens through intimate relationship, He (God) will give you (Jerome) passions and pursuits in His will, in exchange for passions and pursuits that are of your own."

One passionate pursuit of mine that I've always had is that of singing. I love music and really love to sing. I am a fan of many genres of music most notably the big band sound that I inherited from my mom. When I became pastor, of course, we had a choir and I just couldn't help myself every now and then joining in worship. Today, the joy I feel when expressing my love for God through songs of praise is as strong as it has ever been.

Let me tell you what my God has done for me. He has allowed me the opportunity to be a part of the worship arts ministry of my church as a vocalist. I am blessed to be among a talented group of believers who humbly love Jesus and serve the Body of Christ with their talents and gifts. God has been so good to me.

Again, let me remind you of what God desires. 1) That all men might be saved. 2) That we love one another. 3) That we make a difference and. 4)That we reach our full potential and be the best we can be for Him and others, all to His glory!

> ***God has shown me that there is***
> ***more work to be done for Him.***

My desire from this time forward is doing what He has set before me to do. I thank God in advance for granting me the following ministry opportunities to serve:

<u>In the Body of Christ, loving God's people, and preparing them for Kingdom Purpose ...</u>

My HOPE is that He will grant me more opportunities that I might do the work of an Evangelist in equipping believers in the Body of Christ to share the Good News of Jesus Christ.

In return of Him granting my desire, I PROMISE that:

I will GIVE the most efficient service of which I am capable and render the fullest possible quantity and quality in the capacity of Teacher and Evangelist. I will GIVE the best that I have to offer in faithfully sharing His Word, protecting against false doctrine, loving His people, and living before them as an example of Christ in humble service. I will GIVE the Body of Christ, the best that I have to offer in providing biblical instruction on how to share their faith.

I SEE by FAITH, the Word of God being taught and the people of God being engaged and excited about His Word, discovering His will for their lives. I SEE by FAITH, the various ministries being trained, actively growing, and making a difference in the lives they touch and serve. I SEE by FAITH, children and youth, (our future generations), worshiping God and being trained in serving Him and the community. I SEE by FAITH, churches of disciples who are making an impact in the lives of others. I SEE by FAITH, the Kingdom of God expanding because believers in the churches God have given me to serve are sharing their faith, and people are being saved, baptized, and living for God.

<u>In My Career to make a difference in the lives of young people:</u>

My HOPE is to develop positive relationships with Administration, Teachers, Students, and Parents and that I shall be able to use the gifts, talents, and resources God has given me to assist in the growth and development of young people.

In return of Him granting my desires, I PROMISE that:

I will GIVE the best that I have to offer in being a positive role model to youth, inspiring them to strive for excellence in all they do, and challenging them to become who God has created them to be. I will GIVE the most efficient service of which I am capable in the capacity as a Teacher and Mentor.

I SEE by FAITH, a program designed to provide the development of tomorrow's leaders. I SEE by FAITH, my gaining of knowledge, expertise, and training to satisfy my employer's requirements, the needs of my students, and each of us being part of a team. I SEE by FAITH opportunities to share my faith with others and to model before them God's grace. I SEE by FAITH, opportunities to use my skills as a Speaker, and through inspiration, strategically minister to the spiritual needs of others, ALL to GOD'S GLORY.

<u>In My Business equipping others to reach their God-given potential:</u>

I am thankful and my heart is overjoyed with knowing God has given me unique gifts that will add value, help others discover their potential and purpose in life, and lead others to the saving knowledge of Jesus Christ.

In return of Him granting my desires, I PROMISE that:

I will GIVE the best that I have to offer in preparation of providing a service, diligently research subjects of interest in meeting the needs of my clients, and continue to improve my personal growth. I will

GIVE the most efficient service of which I am capable in the capacity of a Trainer, Speaker, and Service Provider.

My HOPE is to minister and provide ongoing training and speaking opportunities in areas that will Educate, Equip, and Empower peoples' lives. I will GIVE the best that I have to offer in meeting the needs of clients and continuing to improve my personal development.

My FAITH is so strong that I can now see myself speaking before audiences both large and small and facilitating workshops and seminars to groups of individuals, churches, and businesses. I SEE by FAITH, a demand for these services and ministries I have to offer.

**Then the LORD replied: "Write down the revelation and make it plain on tablets so that a herald may run with it."
Habakkuk 2:2**

Ask and it shall be given. Seek and ye shall find.
Knock and the door shall be opened.
Matthew 7:7

<u>**I CAN**</u> do all things through Christ who strengthens me.
Philippians 4:19

<u>**I WILL**</u> fulfill my purpose and destiny God had in mind for me.
Jeremiah 29:11

<u>**I MUST**</u> bring GOD glory through my life Matthew 5:16 c

THIS IS MY DESIRE, BE IT THE LORD'S WILL …

LOVE

A friend loves at all times and a brother

(or sister) is born for adversity

Proverbs 17:17

10

JUST FRIENDS

In 1994, a question was asked by my late wife, Helene, whether I would be able to be both the pastor of a church and the director of another ministry, both being full-time vocations. My response to her was, *"Yes, because I have God and you to help me."* It was not easy, but she stuck with me through the good, bad, and the ugly. After all, that's what friends do, right?

It was back sometime around 2002 through a church fellowship with my brother and friend, Pastor Rodger Hunt, and Day Spring Baptist Church that I first met Yolanda, who was a member of that church. She vividly remembers that fellowship meeting when Open Door Gospel Tabernacle came as guests and I preached. I did not see her again for a couple of years when she inquired about volunteering at the Open-Door Rescue Mission working with our Women's Ministry.

From my book, *God's Purpose for My Pain,* I shared how God had sent "angels" my way who ministered to me in unique ways during my time of grieving. Looking back, Yolanda was one of those angels. She was a true friend, someone whose shoulder I could cry on. I was able to be transparent and open my heart to her. I loved and missed my wife, Helene, and Yolanda knew it. Even now, though Yolanda and I are married, it's all right if I say to her, ***"Honey, today I had one of those moments again about Helene."*** Because she is comfortable in her own skin, knows who she is, and what she means to me, if necessary, she would wipe the tears from my eyes and simply smile."

Her sympathy back then was genuine, heartfelt, and comforting. At one particular time I was really hurting with guilt because I missed some signs during Helene's final days that I believed I possibly could have prevented her death. Yolanda reassured me that there was nothing I could have done. I will forever cherish this time Yolanda was there for me. Yolanda has a servant's heart and started to come to the Open Door Rescue Mission to volunteer. She became very helpful to the ministry during this time as we were planning its 60th Anniversary Celebration.

One day my administrative assistant at the mission became very ill and needed to be absent from work for a period of time. Yolanda, who was more than qualified, was there to fill in for her. As previously mentioned, I was not looking for a wife, however, God had something else in mind for me. He began revealing some inner qualities Yolanda possessed that confirmed to me the reason she was there. God knew back then that my greatest need would not be an administrative assistant for the work but a partner for life.

BUT GOD!

When Helene passed in 2009, the reality of no longer having her by my side became very apparent as I found myself trying to go on without her in fulfilling my calling and purpose. There was one time in particular in June 2010 that the weight and burden of ministry was just overwhelming. I felt very depressed, and needed to get away, even if it was just for a few days.

A cousin of Yolanda's who lived in Mississippi was getting married. Yolanda and her father were driving down for the wedding, and I asked if I could go with them. Unfortunately, there was not enough room in the car because Dad (Mr. Magee then), always packed the car with goodies to take home to family members. I was desperate and suggested to Yolanda that if her father was willing to fly, I would purchase the ticket. He agreed and I drove down with her to the wedding. When I met her family, I was amazed at how large it was. I was introduced as "just a friend," which at the time was accurate. Her Aunt Ruth later told her "He's a keeper." Smart woman! The truth be told, even though at the time Yolanda was not on my radar, it was I who needed to keep "her."

As we got to know each other better, she shared her dreams and goals with me. She had been unemployed for a while and desired to seek career opportunities in other states. She asked me to pray on her behalf concerning this. Friends want what's best for friends, and I said I would pray for her. God is faithful, and He hears the prayers of His people. As I began to know her more, I realized that this might be one prayer I did not want to pray, let alone God grant. Needless to say, I am extremely grateful for the outcome.

The more time we spent together, the more attracted I became to her beautiful spirit. I loved the way she made me feel just being around her. Even now, she may want me to go shopping with her, and as much as I am not thrilled about shopping, just spending time with her makes my heart joyful.

It came to me as no surprise that temptation would rear its ugly head during this early time getting to know Yolanda. Those of you who have met her know she is a very beautiful and attractive woman. I noticed it too. I admit, I became physically attracted to her as well, but thanks be to God, she was a woman of God with moral values who believed in and practiced celibacy. What's even more awesome was her concern that I, as a Man of God, not sin before God. A true friend is always looking out for the best interests of their friend. I appreciated her conviction in this matter and that she was looking out for us both.

There has no temptation taken you but such as is common to man
but God is faithful, who will not suffer you to be tempted
above that you are able; but will with the temptation
also make a way to escape, that you
may be able to bear it.
1 Corinthians 10:13

This laid the right foundation for us and is what marriage should be built upon, God's Design.

NEVER LOWER the BIBLICAL STANDARDS of GOD'S WORD.

What we have now is the result of a good foundation that was first established as a friendship. Friends have mutual interest in something. Our mutual interest was that we both loved God and desired to please Him.

Can two walk together, except they be agreed?
Amos 3:3

The Word of God describes true friendship as when one will be honest even when it hurts.

Wounds from a friend can be trusted, but
an enemy multiplies kisses.
Proverbs 27:6

Ecclesiastes 4:9-12 says that **"two are better than one.** And if one prevails against him, two shall withstand him; and a threefold cord is not quickly broken."

Life is so much better when you have a friend in your corner and you don't have to face the challenges of life alone. I first have a friend in Yolanda who I know is with me every step of the way. There is neither an obstacle that we cannot overcome nor a barrier that can stand in our way.

LOVE

Whoso findeth a wife findeth
a good thing and obtaineth
favor of the LORD
Proverb 18:22

11

THE TWO BECAME ONE

I am now a firm believer that lightning can strike twice in the same place. For a person to find true love in life is one of the most remarkable and blessed things one can experience. For it to happen twice, all I can say is, "Thank You Jesus!" To have someone to share life with is amazing and something to be cherished, grateful and appreciated.

I have been truly blessed of God. As shared in my first book, Helene, was a remarkable woman of God. As one who loved God, lived for God, whose hope was in God, she is now with God. No longer would she have to experience the pain and challenges this life brought. She now is experiencing the joy and promise God made to her by accepting His son Jesus as Savior.

> Absent from the body is to be present with the Lord.
> 2 Corinthians 5:8

The reality of this blessing in God keeping his word to our loved ones who have placed their trust in Him is heaven's gain but our loss. I missed my wife greatly and did not know what I would do after she was gone. We had been together since we were young teenagers.

During this time, I realized that I had not only lost her but also an intimacy with God. For some time, I had been going through the motions of ministry. God had to help me realize what had happened.

If a man say I love God, and hateth his brother, he is a liar:
for he that loveth not his brother whom he hath seen
how can he love God whom he hath not seen?
1 John 4:20

An intimate relationship with another woman would not be nearly as precious as it once was until an exclusive intimate relationship with God was what it ought to be. We often try to fill a void in our lives with things that only God can fill. **God is about relationships.** Even from the beginning he established its importance for man.

And the Lord said, "It is not good that man shall be alone
I will make him an help meet for him.
Genesis 2:18

In my previous book, I shared how God spoke to me that time I felt alone and in need of companionship. Even though I began feeling this need, God said wait …

"Not until you're satisfied, fulfilled, and content with being loved by Me <u>alone</u>; with giving yourself totally and unreservedly to Me <u>alone</u>;

to having an intensely personal relationship with Me <u>alone</u>; discovering that only in Me is your satisfaction to be planned for you.

*You will never be united with another until you are united with Me – exclusive of anyone or anything else, exclusive of any other desires or longings. I want you to stop planning, stop wishing, and allow Me to give you the most thrilling plan existing, one that you cannot imagine. I want you to have the best. **<u>Please allow Me to bring it to you</u>**. You just keep watching Me, expecting great things. Keep experiencing the satisfaction that I AM. Keep listening to and learning the things I tell you. You just wait … that's all.*

Don't look around at the things that others have or that I have given them. Don't look at the things you think you want. You just keep looking off and away up to Me, or you'll miss what I want to show you. And then, when you are ready, I'll surprise you with a love far more wonderful that any you would ever have dreamed. Keep your eyes on Me.

***You see, while I'm working on you, I am working on someone for you.** When you are both satisfied and exclusively with Me, and the life I have prepared for you, then you will be ready for each other and able to experience the love that exemplifies your relationship with Me and thus the perfect love."*

During that time of grieving in my life back in 2009, I experienced God in a way that I had never before. Because God was preparing me and Yolanda to become one flesh, my story is her story, and her story is mine, and so….

I waited, and found a healing strength that only God could give.

But they that wait upon the Lord shall renew their strength.
Isaiah 40:31

I waited, and a sense of serenity came over me.

Rest in the Lord, and wait patiently for him: fret not thyself.
Psalm 37:7

I waited until God brought stability back into my life.

I waited patiently for the Lord: and … he set my feet upon a rock
and established my goings.
Psalm 40: 1-2

I waited, for God to do what He said He would do.

And he … kneeled down, and prayed …
nevertheless, not my will, but thine, be done.
Luke 22: 41, 42

I waited on the Lord but did not have to wait very long. *In God's Purpose for My Pain*, I shared of a time when I was given some wise advice from a dear sister in the Lord, Deborah Daniels, after the loss of her husband. She said, ***"Don't make any important decisions for at least a year. For at least one year, we really are insane."*** It was approximately one year later that God revealed to me, "Yolanda is who I give to you."

When you wake up in the morning and look in the mirror, it is only you who is there. You must do what makes you happy. I say this because so much of our lives are spent trying to please other people, and at the end of the day you will find that you cannot please everyone. We will neglect our own happiness. The most important thing to remember in life is what pleases God and makes you happy.

In spite of some not agreeing or understanding that I needed to move on with my life, I embraced my destiny and accepted this gift from God. She came as a gift. I was totally undeserving of someone like her. Again, I am truly a blessed man. Lightning can strike twice in the same place.

Marriage is a full-time job. You must work at it every day. Even though, be it the Lord's will, we will be celebrating another anniversary soon, there were some challenges early in our marriage we had to face in getting where we are today. Every marriage is different and you have to do what works for you. When you have two individuals who are different in personalities, habits, likes, dislikes, interests, communication style, how finances are viewed, types of music, or how they like their eggs, adjustments are necessary if they are to live as one.

One of the mistakes we can make with people is to want them to be what we want instead of letting them be who they are. One thing I intentionally did when I married Yolanda was not to compare her to Helene. There will never be another Helene just like there will never be another you or me. I once heard someone say, *"I can only be me, for when I last looked, "you" was already taken."*

Another thing is to not have unrealistic expectations of your spouse. This might have been more of my challenge than Yolanda's. Of course, having been married before and for such a long time, I was used to certain things being done a certain way by a certain woman. To expect that of Yolanda would not only be unfair but unrealistic. Most women would not allow that to happen anyway. Needless to say, Yolanda was no exception.

Yolanda was raised in a loving two-parent home. What she saw as an example of a good marriage is what she expected in ours, particularly the role her father played. He took sole responsibility of not only providing for his home but also paying the bills. I, on the other hand, never really involved myself in making sure the bills were paid because Helene had that covered. Yolanda expected this of me. She soon discovered that this was not a strength I possessed and that she would have to do it herself.

We discovered that we had to establish "new norms" in our life. Again, I was once married, and Yolanda had never been married. I was the pastor of a church. Yolanda knew nothing about being the wife of a minister, let alone a pastor. I had two grown children and grandchildren. Need more be said about that?

For Yolanda, it was sharing space with someone else and even giving up a closet for my clothes. She was used to calling her father when something needed to be fixed or repaired. I had to let her know that I was now her protector and provider. For me, it was having my eggs fried hard instead of medium sunny side up, and of course "going shopping" now more than I ever had. It was a reprogramming of habits, totally abandoning preconceived expectations, and even starting our own family traditions.

In my first book, I shared a moment when reality really hit me that Helene was gone. "Lest I Forget" was a special family time we had; Helene, my sons, her mom, and I, meeting at the dining table every Sunday morning for breakfast. I still can see her mom sitting at the head of the table ending her prayer with this …

"When I've done all I can do, receive me somewhere in thy kingdom, Amen."

It is unfortunate that today this tradition of family coming together and spending quality time is lost. This was a fond memory and tradition that we had as a family, but then came a new wife and family. Now it became important and critical that we establish our own traditions. One of them was taking a Christmas portrait with our grandchildren. Yolanda and I began doing this when the twins were 2 years old. In our den are portraits all around the room of the last 8 years. To see how we have grown and changed over the years is truly a blessing. I once told someone that as much as I love my sons, there is a special place in my heart even they cannot touch. That place is where my grandbabies are. Amen from you grandparents out there!

I believe in signs, divine ways that God will reveal His plan and will to us. As I mentioned, we have kept this tradition now going on 8 years, but then something happened that really got our attention. One Christmas we did not take a portrait. It wasn't that we weren't ready, for we actually bought new outfits and made our scheduled appointment at the studio. The reason was that the studio was just too crowded. It would have easily been a four hour wait, and we simply wouldn't do it. In all our years we had never seen it like that. What we did instead was go to a mall, find a large Christmas tree and take some pictures together. We really had a great time with our babies. We embraced what I believe God was saying. **"I WANT TO DO SOME NEW THINGS WITH AND FOR YOU!"**

Every once in a while, God will change some things that we are used to doing to prepare us for doing new things, such is marriage. You must be willing and open to doing new things to "keep that fire burning," and growing. Not only are we to grow and evolve personally, so should our relationships.

As God's ambassador in my house, I will cover Yolanda all the days of my life through my words, examples, character, and deeds. As she and I continue to grow stronger and closer each day, we are seeing more of God in one another.

God has blessed me that I might experience His love through her touch, her smile, her compassion and her unconditional love. I love her and she loves me because He first loved us.

EPILOGUE

How I Made It This Far
Thy word was a lamp unto my feet,
and a light unto my path. Psalm 119:105

1) It was God's Grace and Mercy all the time …

He Knew Me before I Knew Myself
I knew you before I formed you in your mother's womb. Before
you were born, I set you apart and appointed
you as my prophet to the nations.
Jeremiah 1:5

For I know the thoughts I have toward you, saith the Lord; thoughts of
peace and not of evil, to give you an expected end.
Jeremiah 29:11

2) I was reminded that God was sovereign and He had a plan.

So shall my word be that goeth forth out of my mouth, it shall not
return unto me void, but it shall accomplish that which

I please, and it shall prosper in the thing whereto I sent it.
Isaiah 55:11

My God, my God, why hast thou forsaken me? Why art thou so far
from helping me and from the words of my roaring? But thou art holy,
O thou that inhabitest the praises of Israel.
Psalm 22:13

And we know that all things work together for good to them that love
God, to them who are the called according to his purpose.
Romans 8:28

3) Friends were there when I needed them

.... a time to keep silence, a time to speak.
Ecclesiastes 3:7

4) I Could Not Have Made It Without ...

My Family

And whether one member suffer, all members suffer with it; or
one member be honored, all members rejoice with it.
Now ye are the body of Christ and
members in particular.
1 Corinthians 12:26-27

My Pastor
(Helene's Eulogy)

For our light affliction, which is but for a moment, worketh for us a
far more exceeding and eternal weigh of glory. While we look not at
the things which are seen but at the things which are not seen: for the
things which are seen are temporal;
but the things which are not seen are eternal.
2 Corinthians 4:17-18

My Friends
My God will supply all your needs according to his glorious
riches in glory by Christ Jesus.
Philippians 4:19

God's Promise
(No matter what life might bring, there is always hope)
If there be no resurrection from the dead, then Christ is not risen:
And if Christ be not risen, then is our preaching in vain and your faith
is also in vain.
1 Corinthians 15: 13-14

For he hath said, I will never leave thee nor forsake thee.
Hebrew 13:5b

Somebody Praying for Me
(Even when I couldn't pray)
The effectual fervent prayer of a righteous man availeth much.
James 5:16

Likewise, the Spirit also helpeth our infirmities: for we know not

what we should pray for as we ought: but the Spirit itself maketh
intercession for us with groanings which cannot be uttered.
27And he that searcheth the hearts knoweth what is the mind of
the Spirit, because he maketh intercession
for the saints according to
the will of God.
Romans 8:26-27

5) I turned my pain over to God

Cast your cares upon me, for I carest for you.
1 Peter 5:7

The angel of the Lord encamps around
those who fear him and he delivers them.
Psalm 34:7

When I felt I could not make it, God was all I needed

Jesus said to me, "My grace is sufficient for you, for my power is made
perfect in weakness." … That is why, for Christ sake, I delight in
weaknesses, in insult, in hardship, in persecutions
in difficulties. For when I am weak then I am strong.
2 Corinthians 12:9-10

The Lord your God is with you, he is mighty to save. He will take
great delight in you he will quiet you with his love he will
rejoice over you with singing.
Zephaniah 3:17

6 When My Breakthru Began …

But they that wait upon the Lord shall renew their strength they shall mount up with wings as eagles; they shall run and not be weary they shall walk and not faint.
Isaiah 40:31

And I will make of you a great nation and I will bless you
(with abundant increase of favors)
and make your name famous and distinguished and you will be a blessing. (dispensing good to others)
Genesis 12:2 AMP

So glad I know Jesus

But I would not have you to be ignorant, brethren concerning them which are asleep, that ye sorrow not even as others which have no hope.
Thessalonians 4:13

But as it is written, Eye hath not seen, nor ear heard Neither have entered into the heart of man
the things which God hath prepared for them that love him.
1 Corinthian 2:9

When the pain was unbearable
and I needed a hiding place

My heart is sore pained within me: and the terrors of death are fallen upon me. Fearfulness and trembling are come upon me and horror hath overwhelmed me. And I said, oh that I had wings like a dove! For then would I fly away and be at rest.

Psalm 55: 5-6

Have mercy on me, my God, have mercy on me, for in you I take refuge. I will take refuge in the shadow of your wings until the disaster has passed.
Psalm 57:1

7) I Finally Got It

Bless the Lord, O my soul: and all that is within me,
bless his holy name.
Psalm 103:1

8) I Became More Committed

He that spared not his own Son, but delivered him up for us all how shall he not with him also freely give us all things?
Romans 8:32

9) I Made God Top Priority

Seek ye first the kingdom of God, and his righteousness and all these things shall be added unto you.
Matthew 6:33

A Sinner Still
BUT GOD!

Oh that I knew where I might find him! That I might order my cause
before him, and fill my mouth with arguments.
Job 23:3-4

If we confess our sins, he is faithful and just to forgive us our sins, and
cleanse from all unrighteousness
1 John 1:9

But he was wounded for our transgressions, he was bruised for our
iniquities: the chastisement of our peace was upon him; and with his
strips we are healed.
Isaiah 53:5

10) In order to Grow, Suffering was Required

I AM the true vine, and my Father is the husbandman.
Every branch in me that beareth not fruit he taketh away; and every
branch that beareth fruit, he purgeth it,
that it may bring forth more fruit.
John 15: 1-2

That the trail of your faith, being much more precious than of gold that
perisheth, though it be tried with fire, might be found unto praise and
honor and glory at the appearing of Jesus Christ.
1 Peter 1:7

11) I Faced Failure, Stepped Out by Faith, and Tried Something Different

For God hath not given us a spirit of fear, but of power, and of love
and of a sound mind.
2 Timothy 1:7

12) I Developed A Servant Mentality

Who, being in the form of God, thought it not robbery to be equal with
God: But made himself of no reputation and took upon himself the
form of a servant, and was made in the likeness
of men: And being found in the fashion as a man, he humbled himself,
and became obedient
unto death, even the death of the cross.
Philippians 2:6-8

The Son of Man did not come to be served, but to serve.
Mark 10:45

13) I Forgave Myself and then Others

Be ye kind one to another, tenderhearted forgiving one another Even as
God for Christ sake have forgiven you.
Ephesians 4:32

(Satan is a liar)
There is therefore no condemnation to them that are in Christ Jesus
Romans 8:1

14) I Had to Change ....

My Thoughts

As a man thinketh in his heart, so is he.
Proverb 23:7

My Attitude

Do nothing out of selfish ambition or vain conceit. Rather, in humility value others above yourselves, not looking to your own interests but each of you to the interests of the others. In your relationships with one another, have the same mindset as Christ Jesus.
Philippians 2:3-5

My Habits / Routine

As obedient children, do not conform to the evil desires you had when you lived in ignorance.
1 Peter 1:14

My Focus

You will seek me and find me when you seek me <u>*with all your heart.*</u>
Jeremiah 29:13

Because he has <u>focused his love on me,</u> I will deliver him. I will protect him because he knows my name. When he calls out to me, I will answer him. I will be with him in his distress. I will deliver him, and I will honor him.
Psalm 91:14-15

Looking unto Jesus the author and finisher of our faith; who for the joy
that was set before him endured
the cross, despising the shame, and is set down at the right hand of the
throne of God.
Hebrews 12:2

15) By God Saying "NO" to What I Thought I Wanted

(God Knew I Didn't Need What I Asked For)
"And this is the confidence that we have in him,
that, if we ask any thing according to his will, he heareth us:"
1 John 5:14

Having the Appropriate Response to His Will for Me
In <u>everything</u> give thanks: for this is the will of God in Christ Jesus
concerning you.
1 Thessalonians 5:18

16) Make No Mistake, God Did It All!

For by grace are ye saved through faith and that not of
yourselves: it is a gift of God, not of works,
lest any man should boast....
Ephesians 2:8

Not by power nor by might but by my spirit saith the Lord.
Zechariah 4:6

Pull me out of the net that they have laid privily for me
for thou art my strength.
Psalm 31:1

There hath no temptation taken you but such as is common to man; but
God is faithful, who will not suffer you to be tempted above that ye are
able; but will with the temptation
also make a way of escape that ye may be able to bear it.
1 Corinthians 10:13

Greater is he that is in you, than he that is in the world.
1 John 4:4

In Summary …

I have been blessed beyond measure in *MY LIFE.*

I was introduced to Jesus Christ as a young child thanks to my grandmother Lexie. I was raised by loving parents who provided for my every need. I met a girl as a teen who was a Christian, who loved God and was destined to serve Him. I have often testified that much of who I am was because of the tremendous calling God had on "her life." I was blessed being with her. Our life together, began a lifelong journey of Christian commitment, dedication and service.

I have been blessed beyond measure by *MY LABOR*

My life of serving God and people was cultivated and nurtured early in my Christian journey by a loving church family and their support of God's higher calling on my life to become a pastor and missionary. To have been used by God as an instrument of His grace; being His hands, heart and voice in helping others experience His love was a privilege and honor. I am grateful for the gifts of His Spirit that He gave me in building His Kingdom, edifying his church, and helping others discover their significance and purpose in life.

I have been blessed beyond measure through ***MY LOVE***

The love I have first came from God. It was His love I experienced in my heart because of Jesus' great love for me. I would not know what love is, had it not been for Calvary.

> *No greater love than this that a man*
> *would lay down his life for a friend.*
> *John 15:13*

My love expressed to my family; Yolanda, Gene, my grandchildren, siblings, brothers and sisters in Christ, those who supported me down through the many years of service, and even those who were against me, is a testament of God's goodness. The love I received from others is what inspired me to believe in myself and the plan God had for my life.

I have come this far because of my faith in God, His love for me, His Spirit in me, and the promises He made in His Word concerning me. I am thankful to God for now the last 14 years and the process I had to go through in order to be where I am. I look forward with great hope, anticipation and expectation of what He has in store for me. I have been ushered into a powerful process that has given me a fruitful life, and I am eternally grateful. I am able to speak boldness into my life:

I am not ashamed: for I know whom I have believed
and am persuaded that he is able to keep that
which I have committed unto
him against that day.
2 Timothy 1: 12

My Prayer…

Lord, help me: To be that husband that deep down I know I can be for Yolanda because she has been a blessing and a gift from YOU that I shall always cherish. To be the good father and grandfather that deep down I know I can be for my son and grandchildren because of how YOU have nurtured and cared for me. To be that Spiritual Leader that deep down I know I can be for YOUR people because of the love I have for them and the gifts YOU have given me to serve, admonish, and care for them. To be that brother and friend that deep down I know I can because of my inheritance with JESUS and the relationship, I have with YOU through HIM. Lord, help me to be that Teacher/Mentor that deep down I know I can be for both the old and young that YOU have placed in my life because of the path YOU have taken me in my personal growth and development.

May all that is accomplished in my life from this time forward bring glory to YOU. I don't know what the future holds, God, but I do know that YOU are forever in it. Because YOU are there, my future is bright! My prayer is for God's blessings and favor to be with you, my friend, as it has been with me. May our lives be pleasing in His sight that one day we will all hear,

"Well done thou good and faithful servant!"

About the Author

Jerome G. Farris is the President and Founder of Destiny Development Design, a 501©3 non-profit that as a Christian company serves the Body of Christ and community, providing quality service in the areas of personal growth, leadership development, and youth enrichment. Through multiple platforms of speaking, training, and coaching, his goal is to educate, equip, and empower others in reaching their full potential.

A special place has grown in his heart for children with autism. This has given birth to a ministry providing Respite Care Family Services, supporting parents and caregivers. The love of his life is his wife, Yolanda. They have one son, Jerome Eugene and three grandchildren; Jerome Douglas, Gabriella, and Chloe.

www.destinydevelopmentdesign.org